MW00844663

ARM Assembly for Embedded Applications

Daniel W. Lewis

Copyright © 2016 by Daniel W. Lewis

All rights reserved. This book or any portion thereof
may not be reproduced or used in any manner whatsoever
without the express written permission of the author
except for the use of brief quotations in a book review.

Printed in the United States of America

First Printing, 2016

ISBN XXX-X-XXXXXXX-X-X

Author Contact Information:

Daniel W. Lewis
Associate Professor
Computer Engineering
Santa Clara University
500 El Camino Real
Santa Clara, California 95053

CONTENTS

PREFACE

This book is about programming in ARM assembly language within the context of embedded applications. The text presents assembly the way it is most commonly used in practice - to implement small, fast, or special-purpose routines called from a main program written in a high-level language such as C. The ARM processor was chosen as the target platform because it is the most prevalent processor for the vast number of embedded applications, including cell phones, tablet computers, disk drives, etc.

The book covers binary number systems, programming using regular integer arithmetic, saturating integer arithmetic, floating-point arithmetic, arithmetic using fixed-point real numbers, an inline coding. In addition, there is extensive treatment of bit manipulation, shifting, extracting and inserting data that is stored in a packed format and material on programming peripheral devices.

INTENDED AUDIENCE

This book is intended for university and community college undergraduate majors, most likely at the sophomore level, who are pursuing a degree in Computer Science, Computer Engineering, or Electrical Engineering and who have completed an introductory programming sequence that includes data structures and programming in a modern high-level language such as C, C++, Java, or Python.

OBJECTIVE

The primary goal of this text is to get students engaged as early as possible. Rather than spending several weeks going over the architecture and detailed instruction set of the processor before having them write programs, the text gets students programming very early by introducing the C/Assembly interface (i.e., function call, parameter passing, return values, register usage conventions) before going into arithmetic, bit manipulation, making decisions, or writing loops. Example functions are presented starting in Chapter 3 and every chapter thereafter. Programming assignments are supported by a free Integrated Development Environment that runs under Microsoft Windows and a library and project template, including support for displaying text, measuring CPU clock cycle times, drawing graphics, and responding to the touch screen of the target platform.

The material is divided into chapters, some of which may be omitted. The first chapter is a brief introduction and the second could be skipped if students already know binary representation of integers. Chapter 8 on multiplication and division tricks, chapter 9 on floating-point, chapter 10 on fixed-point real numbers, and chapter 11 on inline coding may be treated by instructors as elective chapters.

ACKNOWLEDGEMENTS

This book would not have been possible without the efforts of a number of people. Of them all, I owe a special thanks to the students and teaching assistants of COEN 20 at Santa Clara University whose experience in the course has helped to focus and fine-tune the organization and presentation of the material in the book.

I also owe a debt of gratitude to many of my colleague - to Moe Amouzgar for enduring the unenviable task of teaching from my materials and who graciously suggested a number of improvements, and to Darren Atkinson for his invaluable insights and expertise in C, assembly, and compilers.

Finally, I'd like to thank Santa Clara University for granting me the sabbatical leave that made it possible to find the time to complete the text and to Godfrey Mungal, Dean of Engineering, for his financial support during the preparation of the text.

CHAPTER 1
INTRODUCTION

Most modern computers (including the ARM processor used throughout this book) use a design derived from the "stored program" computers[1] that first appeared in the mid 1940's. Initially, there were no high-level languages, compilers, assemblers, or editors. Programmers had no choice but to write their programs in the only language their computers understood - a binary coded representation in which instructions were represented by a sequence of 1's and 0's. Programs were written using paper and pencil, and entered into memory by hand using push buttons and switches. The process involved an incredible amount of detail and was inherently tedious and error-prone. It wasn't until 1949 that the process began to be automated with the introduction of the first rudimentary assembler[2].

At the machine level, a computer program is a sequence of instructions, each consisting of a primitive operation (such as addition, multiplication, etc.) and its operands. Before the introduction of assemblers, programmers had to write each instruction using the binary code of an operation (an "opcode") and the binary address of an operand. Assemblers simplify programming by replacing binary opcodes by easily remembered text mnemonics (e.g., "ADD") and by allowing the programmer to use an identifier (e.g., "mph") to refer to an operand. The assembler keeps track of operand addresses, translates

---

1 Stored program computers were the first to use a single physical memory for both program instructions and data.

2 An excellent history of the development of assemblers can be found in Salomon. *Assemblers and Loaders*, available on the Web at http://www.davidsalomon.name/assem.advertis/asl.pdf.

the opcode mnemonic and operand identifier into their equivalent binary representations, and combines them to form the binary coded representation of an instruction.

1.1 WHY YOU SHOULD LEARN ASSEMBLY

With so many high-level languages available such as C, C++, Java and Python, programming in assembly might seem to be a thing of the past. Indeed, for most applications assembly isn't necessary, or even desirable. Of course those high-level languages wouldn't be possible without compilers, and creating a compiler for a new language or a new processor requires knowing how to produce correct and efficient assembly language or machine code. Even though you may never write a compiler, learning assembly will make you a better high-level language programmer.

Every programming language provides a number of data types, and we are taught that each imposes certain limits on range and precision. While we can simply accept these limitations as fact, programming in assembly brings us closer to their binary representation that causes these limitations and increases our sensitivity to their consequences. For example, a better understanding of data types helps explain why the C expression x>-1 is never true if x is unsigned, although at first it may seem that it should be. Having a better understanding informs and improves our selection of data types for variables, helping to avoid computational errors while promoting the conservation of memory.

Learning assembly helps us see how certain high-level language features are implemented and better understand how they work. For example:

❏ Pass by value prevents functions from modifying actual parameters while pass by reference makes modification possible. Seeing how pass by value and pass by reference are implemented in assembly helps us better understand their semantics.

❑ Languages like C make extensive use of pointers and indirect references, but new C programmers usually struggle with even the simplest of pointer expressions. Diagrams help, but nothing is more illuminating than converting that expression to assembly and tracing through its execution one processor instruction at a time.

❑ In multithreaded programming, we learn that data corruption may occur when two threads access shared data. Knowing assembly helps us understand that the width of that data in bits[3] relative to the maximum width of operands processed in a single instruction[4] can sometimes determine if such data corruption is even possible.

Assembly language teaches us about the components of a computer and how the hardware is designed to optimize performance. The principle of locality of reference predicts that recently accessed data (as well as nearby data, such as the elements of an array) is likely to be used again in a very short period of time. This is the rationale behind the design of memory hierarchies that migrate such data from main memory into a faster cache memory to reduce access time. Understanding the memory hierarchy encourages algorithms that use short code sequences to access a small number of related items rather than long code sequences with reference to a large number of independent variables.

---

[3] A "bit" is a binary digit whose value is either 0 or 1.

[4] The number of operand bits processed in a single instruction is known as "processor word size". For example, a 32-bit processor can add two 32-bit operands in a single instruction.

During the execution of a program, each instruction must be fetched, decoded and executed. The vast majority of these instructions are retrieved from sequentially increasing memory addresses. Memory access for instruction fetch thus represents a special form of locality of reference called spatial locality. Computers exploit this behavior using a hardware design feature called instruction pipelining that significantly increases the rate at which instructions can be processed. For example, pipelining in the ARM processor overlaps the execution of the current instruction with the decoding of the second and the fetch of the third, and effectively triples the rate of instruction processing. However, any branch instruction used to repeat a loop or to make a decision incurs an extra delay because the "pipe" must be flushed and refilled with instructions from the destination of the branch. This is why unrolling a loop into a long sequence of straight line code can be an effective way of improving performance when the resulting increase in program size is not particularly critical.

1.2 WHEN ASSEMBLY IS NEEDED

Assembly language allows us to overcome limitations inherent in a high-level language. For example, arithmetic with very large integers can lead to unexpected errors. In math, multiplying two N-digit operands produces a product of up to 2N digits (e.g., 99x99=9801). Thus a processor instruction designed to multiply two 32-bit integers produces a 64-bit product. Similarly, the corresponding integer divide instruction uses a 64-bit dividend and a 32-bit divisor to produce a 32-bit quotient. However, high-level languages usually define the data type computed by multiplication and division to be the same as that of their operands; e.g., if a and b are 32-bit integers, then so is the value of a*b - meaning that the code produced by a 32-bit C compiler only keeps the least-significant 32 bits of the product. Evaluating the expression (a*b)/c when the values of integers a, b, and c are large may thus produce an incorrect result even though the correct result would fit in a 32-bit integer. Promoting the operands to 64-bit representations produces the correct result, but at a considerable cost in execution time because multiplication and division of 64-bit operands on a 32-bit processor requires calling library functions that execute relatively complex algorithms to perform the computations. A much faster alternative is to write a couple of very small functions in assembly that simply encapsulate the intrinsic multiply and divide instructions and then call these functions from the high-level language program.

Almost anything can be programmed in a high-level language, but sometimes only at the expense of performance or program size. Although compiler optimization technology is quite good, compiled code sometimes has a larger memory footprint and slower performance than is achievable in assembly. Consider the following examples:

❏ A common design goal of many consumer products is to minimize product cost, forcing the use of an inexpensive processor and a very small amount of memory. For example, the software found in one portable CD player used an 8-bit processor with only 32 kilobytes of program storage and 512 bytes of data storage[5]. To achieve reasonable performance within these constraints demands the use of assembly to efficiently implement those parts of the code that have the highest impact on speed or storage.

❏ Network software must frequently reverse the order of bytes[6] in 16-bit and 32-bit data. Fast Fourier Transform (FFT) algorithms require the reversal of bits. Perform-

---

[5] H. Takada, *Designing Embedded Systems with μITRON Kernel*, Embedded Systems Conference, Spring 1998.

[6] A "byte" is a fundamental unit of storage consisting of eight bits.

ing these operations in a high-level language requires several lines of code. However, embedded processors designed for these applications have special bit and byte reversal instructions that can only be used in assembly, providing a solution that runs an order of magnitude faster.

❑ The 2D and 3D graphics of hand-held gaming devices requires a large number of complex computations with real numbers. Most of the processors used in these devices have no machine instructions for floating-point arithmetic. Rather than simulate floating-point instructions using a large and slow software library, these devices instead use a fixed-point representation of real numbers. This allows the basic arithmetic operations for real numbers to be implemented with a set of small and very efficient functions written in assembly using the standard instructions for integer arithmetic with excellent run-time performance.

❑ Most high-level programming languages have no syntax support for low-level access to the hardware of I/O devices and instead require programmers to call library functions. As a result, most device drivers (low-level code that provides direct control of an I/O device) are usually written in assembly.

Finally, knowing assembly language is imperative if you need to reverse engineer malware such as viruses, trojans, adware, spyware and worms. The source code of malware is rarely if ever available, so the only way to protect against it is to first disassemble the binary code and examine the instruction sequences to understand what it does.

1.3 WHAT ASSEMBLY LANGUAGE LOOKS LIKE

Although details vary from one assembler to another, they all share certain common features. Unlike most modern high-level programming languages, assembly language is line-oriented, meaning that each command appears on a line by itself. Blank lines are ignored.

Listing 1-1 is an example of an assembly language source code file written for the GNU assembler that is part of the EmBitz Integrated Development Environment (IDE) used in this book. Comments begin with a pair of forward slashes like in C; the slashes and all text from there to the end of the line are ignored by the assembler.

```
            .syntax      unified
            .cpu         cortex-m4
            .text
            .thumb_func
            .align       2

// int64_t Mult32x32(int32_t mpier, int32_t mcand)

// Input Parameters:    R0 = mpier, R1 = mcand (32-bits each)
// Return Value:        R1.R0 = 64-bit product

            .global      Mult32x32

Mult32x32:  SMULL        R0,R1,R0,R1 // R1.R0 <-- R0*R1
            BX           LR          // Return

            .end
```

Listing 1-1 Example of an assembly language source code file

Other than comments and blank lines, each line of an assembly language program is either a machine instruction or an assembler directive. Assembler directives usually begin with a period (e.g., .align) to distinguish them from the opcode mnemonic of a machine instruction (e.g., SMULL). Each such line consists of three fields separated by whitespace - the label field, a field used for either a directive or an opcode mnemonic, and a list of one or more operands separated by commas. Instructions that leave a result in a register, or that copy the contents of a register into memory, list that register as the first operand in the list[7].

The label field is optional; if present, the label must begin in column one, follow the usual rules for identifiers[8], and be terminated with a colon. Labels are often case sensitive, while directives, opcode mnemonics, and operands are usually *not* case sensitive.

The ARM processor is used in a large variety of embedded applications, including cell phones, tablet computers, handheld game consoles, GPS navigation devices, digital cameras, media players, and disk drives. Most of the software for these devices is written in a language like C, supported by a small number of functions written in assembly language. Assembly is used only as needed to overcome limitations in the syntax of the high level language, to provide efficient access to low-level hardware features, and to optimize performance. In this context, the functions written in assembly (like the one shown in Listing 1-1) tend to have only a few input parameters and contain a comparatively small number of instructions.

1.4 HOW ASSEMBLERS WORK

In an assembly language program, labels are attached to instructions or data definitions so that their memory location can

---

[7] There are a few instructions that leave their result in a *pair* of registers or that copy the content of a pair of registers to memory. These instructions list these registers as the first two in the operand list.

[8] Identifiers must consist of upper and lowercase letters, digits, and underscores and must start with either a letter or an underscore.

be referenced from other parts of the program. The purpose of an assembler is to replace each such reference by the numeric address that it refers to. To do this, the assembler has to make two passes over the source code. During the first pass, the assembler builds a *symbol table* containing all of the identifiers and their address values, and then uses the information in the table during the second pass to make the replacements.

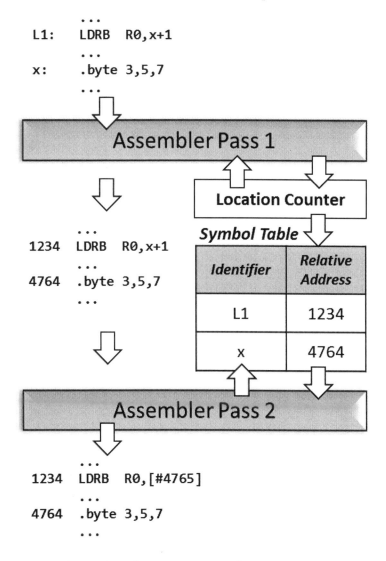

Figure 1-1 The two passes of an assembler.

While reading through the source code during the first pass, the assembler uses a variable called the *location counter* to keep track of addresses. As each line of text is read, the assembler adds a constant to the location counter, corresponding to the number of bytes occupied by the instruction or data definition. In this way, the location counter always contains the relative address of the next line of source code and thus the address value to enter into the symbol table when it finds a label starting in column one.

Each instruction must ultimately be converted into a binary representation partitioned into fields of bits – one bitfield to specify the operation to be performed (the opcode), and others that specify the operands. For example, the binary representation of the LDRB instruction in Figure 1-1 contains three bitfields – one to specify the opcode, a second to specify the register, and a third to specify a memory address.

It is important to understand that x+1 is an address expression whose value is the address of the second byte (the value 5) of three starting at the address represented by the identifier, x. The addition in x+1 occurs during assembly, <u>not</u> during program execution.

1.5 HARDWARE ENVIRONMENT USED IN THIS BOOK

Our objective is to learn how to program in ARM® assembly language. However, most ARM processors are used in embedded applications that do not have the kind of keyboards, displays, or mouse that we're accustomed to on a desktop or laptop computer. This means we have to use a cross-platform approach in which we edit and compile our program on one computer (typically a PC) and then download it to the program memory of an ARM-based small board computer.

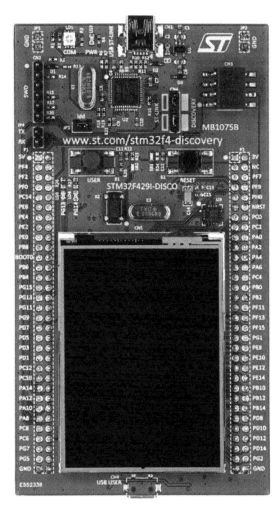

Figure 1-2 STMicroelectronics 32F429I-DISCO Discovery
board. © *STMicroelectronics. Used with permission.*

In this book we will use the EmBitz IDE to develop programs
that run on the STMicroelectronics 32F429I-DISCO Discovery
board shown in Figure 1-2. This inexpensive board uses the
ARM 32-bit Cortex-M4F processor that implements the
Thumb-2 instruction subset of the ARM architecture. The
board also has a 240x320 color display capable of displaying
several lines of text and a standard C software run-time library.
We will explore programming in assembly by writing func-

tions called by a C program. We will use C to write the main program, provide test data, verify results, and format output for the display.

1.6 INTEGER DATA TYPES USED IN THIS BOOK

The size of the traditional integer data types in C varies from one compiler to another. The C99 standard merely specifies their *minimum* sizes: at least 8 bits for a char, at least 16 for a short int, at least 32 for long int, and at least 64 for a long long int. An int with no size qualifier is required to contain at least 16 bits. In fact, a very common compiler variation is whether the int data type is implemented as 16, 32 or 64 bits.

Writing assembly language requires attention to the size of integer operands and whether they are signed or unsigned. In the ARM processor, for example, there are several different instructions for accessing integer variables according to their size and signedness. Therefore, to avoid any ambiguity when creating a program that is a mix of C and assembly, use the new integer data types introduced by the C99 standard[9] that require a specific number of bits in the representation.

---

[9] Note: In order to use the new C99 integer data types, a C program must #include the stdint.h header file.

Table 1-1 New C99 Signed Integer Data Types

Signed Data Types	Exact Size	Use instead of ...
int8_t	8 bits	signed char
int16_t	16 bits	signed short int
int32_t	32 bits	signed int, signed long int
int64_t	64 bits	signed long long int

Table 1-2 New C99 Unsigned Integer Data Types

Unsigned Data Types	Exact Size	Use instead of ...
uint8_t	8 bits	unsigned char
uint16_t	16 bits	unsigned short int
uint32_t	32 bits	unsigned int, unsigned long int
uint64_t	64 bits	unsigned long long int

1.7 IDENTIFIER CONVENTIONS USED IN THIS BOOK

Throughout this book, the identifiers chosen for variables and functions will often reflect their data type, including the number of bits in the representation and whether the value is signed or unsigned.

For example, a signed 32-bit integer variable might be given the name "s32", and an 8-bit unsigned integer might be given the name "u8". Sometimes whether the value is signed or unsigned is irrelevant and an identifier such as "x16" might be

chosen for a variable, or one like "get8" for the name of a function.

While there's no reason to follow this convention when you
create your own programs or functions, it helps to remind the
reader of this book about the importance of choosing the appropriate instruction. For example, there are six different variations of the "Load Register" instruction, corresponding to the
size of its operand and whether the operand contains a signed
or unsigned value. Making the correct choice is one of the
many low-level details that make programming in assembly
language a bit more challenging.

CHAPTER 2
BINARY NUMBER SYSTEMS

When we need a constant, decimal representation is the typical choice, but when manipulating bits and bytes it is usually more appropriate to use other representations, such as binary or hexadecimal (hex). Decimal, binary and hex are all examples of positional number systems in which numbers are written as a sequence of digits from a specified set. The number of digits is determined by the radix (or number base). Since hex has more than ten digits, it uses the first six letters of the alphabet for the last six digits. Each digit should thus be considered as a symbol that stands for a specific numeric value.

Table 2-1 Symbols and their values used in positional number systems.

System	Radix	Digit Symbols	Corresponding Digit Values
Binary	2	0,1	0,1
Decimal	10	0,1,2,3,4,5,6,7,8,9	0,1,2,3,4,5,6,7,8,9
Hex	16	0,1,2,3,4,5,6,7,8,9,A,B,C,D,E,F	0,1,2,3,4,5,6,7,8,9,10,11,12,13,14,15

The discussion of number systems in this text uses a subscript to indicate the radix of a number when needed for clarity. To distinguish binary and hex constants from decimal constants in

ARM assembly however, binary constants are written with a prefix of 0b or 0B (e.g., 0b1011) and hex constants with a prefix of 0x or 0X (e.g., 0x12FC) [10].

Each digit has a weighting factor determined by its relative position in the sequence; together, the numeric values of the digits and their weighting factors determine the magnitude of the number based on a polynomial evaluation. For example, we're all familiar with how positional number systems work in decimal:

$$547_{10} \rightarrow \qquad = 5 \times 10^2 + 4 \times 10^1 + 7 \times 10^0$$
$$= 5 \times 100 + 4 \times 10 + 7 \times 1$$
$$= 500 + 40 + 7$$

This extends in a natural way for decimal numbers that contain fractional digits, as in:

$$9.32_{10} \rightarrow \qquad = 9 \times 10^0 + 3 \times 10^{-1} + 2 \times 10^{-2}$$
$$= 9 \times 1 + 3 \times .1 + 2 \times .01$$
$$= 9 + .3 + .02$$

2.1 CONVERTING UNSIGNED BINARY TO DECIMAL

The only difference in binary is that the weighting factors are powers of 2:

$$1011_2 \rightarrow \qquad = 1 \times 2^3 + 0 \times 2^2 + 1 \times 2^1 + 1 \times 2^0$$
$$= 1 \times 8 + 1 \times 2 + 1 \times 1$$
$$= 8 + 2 + 1$$
$$= 11_{10}$$

---

[10] EmBitz also supports octal numbers, but they are rarely used and will not be covered.

Note that polynomial evaluation provides a convenient way to convert a binary number into its decimal equivalent. Converting a number with fractional digits, however, can lead to several tedious divisions. Consider:

$$10.0101111_2 \rightarrow \; = 1{\times}2^1 + 0{\times}2^0 + 0{\times}2^{-1} + 1{\times}2^{-2} + 0{\times}2^{-3} + $$
$$1{\times}2^{-4} + 1{\times}2^{-5} + 1{\times}2^{-6}$$

$$= 2 + 1/4 + 1/16 + 1/32 + 1/64$$

$$= 2 + 0.25 + 0.0625 + 0.03125 + 0.015625$$

$$= 2.359375_{10}$$

An easier way to handle this is to remove the radix point, convert the number as if it were an integer, and then divide (only once) by 2^k, where k is the number of fractional digits in the original binary number:

$$10.0101111_2 \rightarrow \; = (1{\times}2^7 + 0{\times}2^6 + 0{\times}2^5 + 1{\times}2^4 + 0{\times}2^3 + $$
$$1{\times}2^2 + 1{\times}2^1 + 1{\times}2^0)/2^6$$

$$= (128 + 16 + 4 + 2 + 1)/64$$

$$= 151/64$$

$$= 2.359375_{10}$$

2.2 CONVERTING UNSIGNED DECIMAL TO BINARY

What about going the other way? What if we have an unsigned decimal number and need to know its binary representation? There are essentially two approaches. In the first method, the whole and fractional parts of a decimal number must be converted using different algorithms. The second method has no such requirement. Use whichever method is easier.

2.2.1 Method #1a: Converting the whole part

The following algorithm converts the whole part of an unsigned decimal number N to binary using repeated integer division, producing digits of the whole part of the result in right-to-left order:

Step 1:   Divide N by 2. Output the remainder and re-place N by the quotient.

Step 2:   If N is zero, STOP. Else go to Step 1.

Example: Find the binary representation of 13_{10}

N	Quotient	Remainder	Result
13	6	1	1.
6	3	0	01.
3	1	1	101.
1	0	1	1101.

2.2.2 Method #1b: Converting the fractional part

The following algorithm converts the fractional part of an un-signed decimal number N to binary using repeated multiplica-tion, producing digits of the whole part of the result in left-to-right order:

Step 1:   Multiply N by 2. Output the whole part of the product and replace N by the fractional part.

Step 2:   If N is zero, STOP. Else go to Step 1.

Note: This algorithm may never terminate for some initial val-ues of N. In this case, stop when the result contains the desired number of binary fractional digits. This happens when there is no exact binary representation of the value, similar to there being no exact decimal representation of one-third even though it has an exact base 3 representation (0.1_3).

Example: Find the binary representation of 0.1_{10}

N	Product (2×N)	Whole Part	Fractional Part	Result
.1	0.2	0	.2	.0
.2	0.4	0	.4	.00
.4	0.8	0	.8	.000
.8	1.6	1	.6	.0001
.6	1.2	1	.2	.00011

Note: The next value of N (.2) is the same as the second value in the list, causing the algorithm to repeat indefinitely.

2.2.3 Method #2: Starting with the largest k such that $2^k \leq N$

The following algorithm converts an unsigned decimal number N to binary, producing digits of the result in left-to-right order. While it may seem more complex than the previous approach, many find it easier to use. Essentially, the algorithm chooses the powers of 2 whose sum is the original number.

Step 1:   Find the largest integer k, such that $2^k \leq N$

Step 2:   If $N < 2^k$, output 0.
Else output 1 and replace N by $N - 2^k$

Step 3:   If k = 0, output a radix point

Step 4:   Replace k by k − 1

Step 5:   If N = 0 and k < 0, STOP. Else go to Step 2

Note: As before, the algorithm may never terminate for certain fractional values.

Example: Find the binary representation of 2.75_{10}

Step	N	k	Action	Result
1	2.75	?	The largest k such that $2^k \leq N$ is 1	
2	2.75	1	$N \geq 2^k$, so output 1; $N \leftarrow N - 2^k$	1
3	0.75	1	$k \neq 0$ (continue at Step 4)	
4	0.75	1	$k \leftarrow 1 - 1 = 0$	
5	0.75	0	$k \geq 0$, go to step 2	
2	0.75	0	$N < 2^k$, so output 0	10
3	0.75	0	k=0, so output the radix point	10.
4	0.75	0	$k \leftarrow 0 - 1 = -1$	
5	0.75	−1	$N \neq 0$, so go to step 2	
2	0.75	−1	$N \geq 2^k$: output 1, replace N by $N-2^k$.	10.1
3	0.25	−1	$k \neq 0$ (continue at Step 4)	
4	0.25	−1	$k \leftarrow -1 - 1 = -2$	
5	0.25	−2	$N \neq 0$, go to step 2	
2	0.25	−2	$N \geq 2^k$, so output 1; $N \leftarrow N - 2^k$	10.11
3	0.00	−2	$k \neq 0$ (continue at Step 4)	
4	0.00	−2	$k \leftarrow -2 - 1 = -3$	
5	0.00	−3	N=0 and k<0: STOP	

2.3 SIGNED 2'S COMPLEMENT INTEGERS

Unsigned numbers only provide a way to represent magnitude. Signed numbers that may be either positive or negative require a different binary representation. As humans, we're used to the *sign plus magnitude* representation to write decimal numbers using a magnitude and optional leading plus or minus sign. While computers could be designed to use a binary version of sign plus magnitude, it happens to be much more efficient in hardware to use a different scheme called *2's complement*. As a result, today essentially every computer uses a 2's complement representation of signed numbers.

In 2's complement, the most significant bit is referred to as the "*sign bit*". Unfortunately, that implies (incorrectly) that the sign and magnitude of a number are separate and independent within the representation. The fact that you can determine the sign of a 2's complement number by examining the most-significant bit is merely an observable characteristic of the representation.

An easy way to understand 2's complement is to think of a car with an 8-bit binary odometer. When the car first rolls off the assembly line, the odometer displays 00000000. If you were to drive the car forward, you would see the odometer increase to 00000001 (1 mile), 00000010 (2 miles), 00000011 (3 miles), 00000100 (4 miles), etc. If you were to drive the car for a very long time, eventually the odometer would "roll over" from 11111111 to 00000000 and start over. Normal odometers only record mileage driven as an unsigned value in the forward direction. However, if the odometer displayed a signed mileage and could update in both forward and reverse, then driving backwards from 00000000 should cause the next displayed value to be 11111111 (-1 miles), and then 11111110 (-2 miles), 11111101 (-3 miles), 11111100 (-4 miles), etc.

We can see that there are two ways of *interpreting* the mileage from the *representation* displayed on the odometer. An unsigned interpretation would allow mileages from 00000000 (0 miles) to 11111111 (255 miles). However, we can alternatively interpret the displayed digits as a signed value in which negative values have a 1 in the most-significant digit position, and positive values start with a 0. The total number of displayed values is the same, but the range would be interpreted as 10000000 (-128 miles) to 01111111 (+127 miles).

Remember the notion of a number line in which numbers are placed next to equally spaced points on a line that runs between plus and minus infinity? Computers, like the odometer, use numbers with a fixed number of digits. As a consequence, the number line is has fixed end points; going beyond the last number on either end causes the number to "wrap around" to the other end. This means the number line is more like a number circle. The points around the circle correspond to the natural pattern of a count sequence, increasing in a clockwise direction. However, we may choose to interpret those patterns as representations of signed or unsigned values as shown in Figure 2-1.

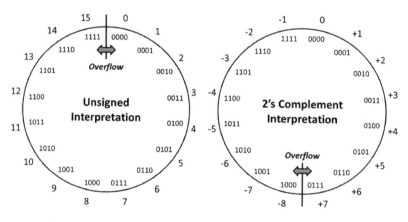

Figure 2-1 Two different interpretations of a 4-bit binary representation.

The range of binary values depends on the number of bits in the representation and whether we use an unsigned or 2's complement interpretation. In either case, a representation with N bits has a total of 2^N different patterns. In an unsigned interpretation, these patterns represent values from 0 to 2^N-1. In a 2's complement interpretation, half of the values are positive and half are negative. Half of 2^N is 2^{N-1}. Thus the range of positive values in an N-bit 2's complement number goes from 0 to $+2^{N-1}-1$, and the range of negative values goes from -1 to -2^{N-1}. For example, the range of 4-bit unsigned values shown in Figure 2-1 is 0 to 15 (2^4-1) and the range of 4-bit 2's complement values is -8 (-2^3) to +7 ($+2^3$-1). In either unsigned or 2'scomplement, going beyond the limits of the range is called an *overflow*.

2.3.1 Converting Decimal to Two's Complement

Suppose we'd like to find the N-bit 2's complement represen-tation of a decimal number.

If the number is positive, simply find the unsigned binary rep-resentation of the magnitude and add <u>one</u> or more 0's on the left until you have a total of N bits. If there's not at least one spare bit position to put a zero at the far left, then the decimal number is outside the range of representation. If the number is negative, first find the N-bit unsigned binary representation of the magnitude. Then convert the representation to that of the equivalent negative number of the same magnitude.

Changing the sign of a two's complement number requires a process that's called "finding the two's complement". There are two ways to do this. Both methods are shown below and used in examples to find the 8-bit representation of -20_{10}:

Method 1: Change every bit (i.e., 0's become 1's and vice-versa) and add 1 (using binary addition):

Unsigned 8-bit representation of 20_{10}:   00010100

Change every bit: 11101011

Add 1:   11101100

Method 2:	Copy the bits from right-to-left, through and including the first 1. Copy the opposite of all the remaining bits:

Unsigned 8-bit representation of 20_{10}:   `00010100`

Copy right-to-left through 1st 1:   `-----100`

Copy the opposite of remaining bits: `11101100`

2.3.2 Converting Two's Complement to Decimal

Given a 2's complement binary number, we find the corresponding decimal value in one of two ways. Both methods are shown below and used in examples to find the decimal value of the 8-bit 2's complement number 10001100:

Method 1:	If the number if positive (most-significant bit is 0), use a polynomial evaluation. If the number is negative, use one of the two algorithms presented in section to find the corresponding positive representation. Apply a polynomial evaluation to it and add a leading minus sign.

Original 2's complement number: 10001100

Negative – find positive equivalent: 01110100

Polynomial evaluation: $64+32+16+4 = 116$

Add a leading minus sign: −116

Warning: This algorithm fails for if the value is full-scale negative (e.g., 10000000).

> Method 2:   Use a polynomial evaluation, but change the weight of the most significant bit to a negative value.

Original 2's complement number: 10001100

Polynomial evaluation: $-128+8+4 = -116$

2.4 HEX AS A SHORTHAND FOR BINARY

It takes fewer hex digits to represent a value than decimal, and far fewer than binary. Writing constants with fewer digits is more convenient and produces fewer mistakes. What really makes hex so appealing, however, is that it is a simple short-hand notation for binary. Conversion from binary to hex or vice-versa can be done by inspection due to the power relation-ship, $16 = 2^4$. This relationship causes each hex digit to corre-spond to exactly four binary digits. In other words, a hex num-ber can be converted to binary one hex digit at a time, with each digit converted to binary independent of the other hex digits. Similarly, a binary number can be organized into groups of four binary digits, and each group converted to a single hex digit independent of the other groups.

Example: Convert the hex number $F12C_{16}$ to binary using Table 2-2.

$F1.2C_{16}$ →   F   1   .   2   C

                        1111   0001   .   0010 1100_2

When converting from binary to hex, be careful to form groups of four bits each working outward starting from the radix point. If the far left group is incomplete, add extra zeroes on the left. Similarly, if the far right group is incomplete, add extra zeroes on the right. Then convert each group to a corresponding hex digit.

Example: Convert the binary number 1011010.1001011_2 to hex.

$1011010.1001011_2 \rightarrow$	101	1010	.	1001	011
	0101	1010	.	1001	0110
	5	A	.	9	6_{16}

These conversions are easy if you memorize Table 2-2. If you have difficultly remembering the binary entries in the table, take note of how the binary digits change from one line to the next: The least-significant binary digit changes on every line, the next digit changes on every second line, etc.

Table 2-2 Hex/Binary Conversion Table

Hex Digit	Binary Equivalent	Hex Digit	Binary Equivalent
0	0000	8	1000
1	0001	9	1001
2	0010	A	1010
3	0011	B	1011
4	0100	C	1100
5	0101	D	1101
6	0110	E	1110
7	0111	F	1111

PROBLEMS

1. Give the entire count sequence of binary patterns for 4-bit unsigned integers. At which transition point does an overflow occur if the patterns represent:
   - (a)   An unsigned integer?
   - (b)   A 2's complement integer?

2. What is the decimal value represented by the $\overset{12}{8}$-bit binary number 11001001.0101_2 when interpreted as:
   - (a)   An unsigned number?
   - (b)   A 2's-complement number?

3. Use polynomial evaluation to convert:
   - (a) 101101_2 to base 10.
   - (b) $DEAF_{16}$ to base 10.

4. Use repeated division to convert:
   - (a) 150_{10} to base 2.
   - (b) 1500_{10} to base 16.

5. Use repeated multiplication to convert:
   - (a) 0.9_{10} to base 2.
   - (b) 0.9_{10} to base 16.

   Note: If the process repeats indefinitely, calculate as few digits as necessary to provide same or better resolution.

6. Use shortcuts based on power relationships to convert:
   - (a) $ACE5_{16}$ to base 2.
   - (b) $FA.CE_{16}$ to base 2.
   - (c) 101011.01101_2 to base 16.

7. Convert the following 2's complement numbers to decimal:
   - (a)   01010101.
   - (b)   10101010.
   - (c)   1000.0001

(d)   1001.0110
(e)   0111.1110

8. Convert the following decimal numbers to 2's complement:
   (a)   −6.7
   (b)   −37.1
   (c)   -100
   (d)   -7.7

9. Find the 2's complement of the following binary numbers:
   (a)   01010101.
   (b)   10101010.
   (c)   1000.0001
   (d)   1001.0110
   (e)   0111.1110

10. Consider a 2's complement number represented by n bits, with two bits to the left of the binary point (e.g., $b_1 b_0 . b_{-1} b_{-2} \cdots b_{(n-2)}$).
    (a)   Give an algebraic expression in terms of n for the <u>positive</u> value that has the smallest non-zero magnitude.
    (b)   Give the binary representation of (a), where n is 8.
    (c)   Give an algebraic expression in terms of n for the <u>negative</u> value that has the smallest magnitude.
    (d)   Give the binary representation of (c), where n is 8.

11. What are the most positive and most negative decimal values of a 6-bit 2's-complement number?

12. What are the minimum and maximum decimal values of a 6-bit unsigned number?

13. Under what condition does adding 1 to a binary integer consisting of all 1's cause an overflow?

14. In 2's complement, are the absolute values of full-scale negative and full-scale positive are identical or not? Explain why.

EXTRA CREDIT

15. Convert:

Same or better resolution if ∞

    (a) 0.324_7 to base 10.
    (b) 400_{10} to base 7.
    (c) 0.9_{10} to base 3.
    (d) 12.34_5 to base 7.
    (e) 35.2_7 to base 10.
    (f) 35.2_{10} to base 7.

16. Use shortcuts based on power relationships to convert:

    (a) $FACE_{16}$ to base 8.
    (b) 1011.0111_2 to base 8.
    (c) 232.1_4 to base 8.
    (d) 17.6_9 to base 3.
    (e) 1100011.11001_2 to base 8.
    (f) 71.3_8 to base 4.

17. The exact binary representation of one-sixth (1/6) requires an infinite number of digits. Truncating it (discarding extra bits) to make it fit within a fixed-precision representation creates a representational error. What is the absolute error that results from storing one-sixth without rounding using 8 fractional bits?

18. What is the minimum number of fractional binary digits required to have at least the same resolution as 3 fractional decimal digits?

PROGRAMMING PROBLEMS

19. Write a C program to convert an 8-bit binary number to a two-digit hexadecimal number, where the binary number is stored in an array of integers, one bit per integer. Test your program for several values.

20. Write a C program to convert a two-digit hexadecimal number to an 8-bit binary number, where the binary number is stored in an array of integers, one bit per integer. Test your program for several values.

21. Write a C program to convert an 8-bit binary number to decimal, where the binary number is stored in an array of integers, one bit per integer. Your program should convert the binary number (1) as if it was unsigned, and (2) as if it was a 2's complement signed number. Test your program for several values, including the minimum and maximum limits of the unsigned and 2's complement ranges.

22. Write a C program to convert a decimal number to an 8-bit binary number, where the binary number is stored in an array of integers, one bit per integer. Your program should create both the 8-bit unsigned and 8-bit 2's complement representations of the decimal number. Test your program for several values, including the minimum and maximum limits of the unsigned and 2's complement ranges.

23. Write a C program to take an 8-bit 2's complement number and form the 2's complement representation of the negative of its value. Both the input number and its negative should be stored as an array of integers, one bit per integer. Test your program for several values, including the minimum and maximum limits of the 2's complement ranges.

CHAPTER 3

WRITING FUNCTIONS IN ASSEMBLY

Our objective is to write functions in assembly that are called by programs written in C. This means that we must implement functions in a way that is compatible with the code that the C compiler generates to call a function, including how it passes parameters and where it expects to find the function result.

The ARM processor has sixteen 32-bit storage locations known as registers R0 through R15, some of which are used to hold function parameters and return values. As we will see, compilers for the ARM processor also require that functions must follow certain standardized rules regarding how they may use these registers.

3.1 FUNCTION CALL AND RETURN

When you call a function, the processor suspends the current instruction sequence, records the address of the instruction immediately following the call (the return address), and then branches to the entry point of the function and begins executing the function. When the function ends, the processor branches back to the return address and resumes the previous instruction sequence.

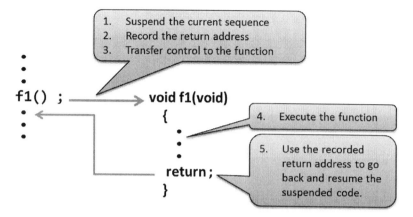

Figure 3-1 Simple function call and return in C

Register R14 of the ARM processor is used to hold the return address during a function call. This register is known as the "Link Register" and is also referred to as register LR. Function calls are implemented using the "Branch with Link" instruction (BL), which records the return address in register LR and then transfers control to the function. When the function returns, it executes a "Branch Indirect" instruction (BX), which transfers control back to the instruction at the address held in LR.

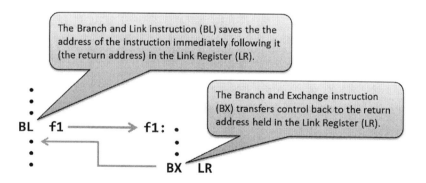

Figure 3-2 Simple function call and return in ARM assembly

Since there is only one Link Register, nested function calls require that the contents of LR be preserved on the stack, using PUSH and POP instructions. These instructions are actually capable of pushing or popping several registers at once. Their operand field is thus a comma-separated *list* of registers, and so must be enclosed in curly braces as shown in Figure 3-3. We will add more registers to the list as our function template develops.

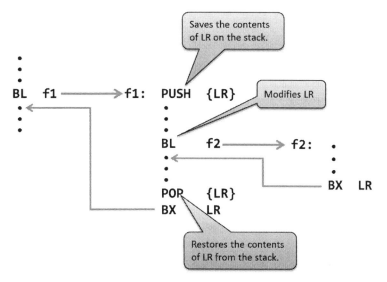

Figure 3-3 Nested function calls must save and restore LR.

3.2 ACCESSING PARAMETERS INSIDE THE FUNCTION

In C, all parameters are passed by value. That means that when the name of a variable appears as an actual argument in a function call, only a copy of its value is provided to the function. Although the function is able to modify the value of the copy, it is impossible for the function to modify the value of the original actual argument.

The compiler implements pass by value as follows: When you call a function in C, the compiler generates code that copies the arguments in left-to-right order into registers R0 through R3 before the BL instruction that calls the function (see Figure 3-4). Once inside an assembly language function, you can only access the arguments by referring to the values that were copied into the registers. Identifiers that appear as variable or formal parameter names in the C program aren't recognized inside the assembly language function.

C Function Call	Compiler Output
int8_t x8 ; int32_t y32 ; int32_t z64 ; • • • foo(x8, y32, z64) ; • • •	• • • LDRSB R0,x8 // R0 <-- x8 LDR R1,y32 // R1 <-- y32 LDRD R2,R3,z64 // R3.R2 <-- z64 BL foo • • •

Figure 3-4 How parameters are passed to a function by the compiler.

8, 16, and 32-bit parameters will each occupy an entire 32-bit register, with 8 and 16-bit values extended to an equivalent 32-bit representation. 64-bit parameters must be copied into a consecutive register pair, with the least-significant half in the first register and the most-significant half in the second. If the number or type of parameters requires more than four registers, the compiler generates code that passes the additional parameters by copying them onto the stack. However, the kind of assembly language functions we are writing rarely needs more than four parameters. When they do, it's usually more efficient to put them in a structure and pass the address of the structure to the function.

3.3 PREPARING THE RETURN VALUE

Most functions in C programs calculate and return a scalar result. When you call such a function the code generated by the compiler expects that result to be left in register R0. For example, in Figure 3-5 the compiler uses a Store (STR) instruction to copy the 32-bit return value from register R0 into the memory location occupied by the 32-bit variable called save32.

C Function Call	Compiler Output

`int32_t get32(void) ;`
`int32_t save32 ;`
 	
•
•
•
`save32 = get32() ;`
 	
•
•
•
	•
	•
	•
	`BL   get32`
	`STR  R0,save32`
	•
	•
	•

Figure 3-5 Retrieving the function return value.

In a 32-bit C compiler, all 8 and 16-bit integers are automatically promoted to an equivalent 32-bit representation before those values are used in expressions. Thus for efficiency reasons, functions designed to return an 8 or 16-bit result are expected to do the promotion *once* inside the function instead of having every function call followed by code to do the promotion. The return value may then be stored from the register into an 8, 16 or 32-bit variable. Promotion to a 64-bit value is rarely needed and so is performed after the return (see Figure 3-6).

C Function Call	Compiler Output
uint8_t save8, get8(void) ; uint16_t save16 ; uint32_t save32 ; uint64_t save64 ; • • • save8 = get8() ; save16 = (uint16_t) get8() ; save32 = (uint32_t) get8() ; save64 = (uint64_t) get8() ; • • •	• • • BL get8 STRB R0,save8 BL get8 STRH R0,save16 BL get8 STR R0,save32 BL get8 LDR R1,=0 STRD R0,R1,save64 • • •

Figure 3-6 Promotion of a function return value from 8 to 16 or 32 bits.

Functions that return 64-bit values are expected to return their result in registers R0 and R1, with the least-significant half of the result in R0 and the most-significant half in R1. For example, in Figure 3-7, the compiler uses a Store Double (STRD) instruction to copy the 64-bit return value from registers R0 and R1 into the memory location occupied by a 64-bit variable.

C Function Call	Compiler Output
int64_t get64(void) ; int64_t save64 ; • • • save64 = get64() ; • • •	• • • BL get64 STRD R0,R1,save64 • • •

Figure 3-7 Function returning a 64-bit integer.

3.4 REGISTER USAGE CONVENTIONS

R0 through R3 are perhaps the most useful of the sixteen ARM registers. Any of these registers that are not used to pass parameters or to hold a function return value may be used as scratch registers to hold temporary values. Any values they may have held prior to calling the function are not expected to still be there after the function returns. Functions may therefore modify their content without preserving their original values. However, this also means that one of these registers can only be used to hold a value until the next function call since that call might modify its content.

Using only R0-R3 and no function call	Using only R0-R3 and calling another function

``text
f1: •
     •   // OK to modify R0-R3
     •
     BX   LR
``
	``text
	f2: PUSH {LR}
	     •
	     • // OK to modify R0-R3
	     •
	     BL f3 // might modify R0-R3
	     •
	     POP {LR}
	     BX LR
	``

Figure 3-8 Functions that modify only registers R0 - R3.

Of course the processor has twelve more registers, but some of these are reserved for special purposes. We've already seen that R14 is used as the Link Register (LR), holding the return address recorded by the Branch and Link (BL) instruction. Register R13 serves as the Stack Pointer (SP) that keeps track of memory locations used by the PUSH and POP instructions. And register R15 is the Program Counter (PC) that holds the address used to fetch an instruction from memory. In addition, some compilers reserve register R12 for the linker to use as an Intra Procedure call scratch register (IP).

That leaves registers R4 through R11 to hold temporary variables. Any function that modifies one of these registers is required to preserve its original content. Otherwise, any modification could destroy information that was in the register before the function call and expected to still be there upon return.

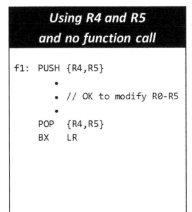

Figure 3-9 Functions that modify (for example) registers R4 and R5.

All of this is summarized in what is known as the Base Standard of the Procedure Call Standard for the ARM Architecture (AAPCS) and appears in Table 3-1. Note that all the registers may be referred to using either R0 through R15 or by their corresponding AAPCS name.

Table 3-1 ARM Architecture Procedure Call Standard (AAPCS)

Register	AAPCS Name	Usage	Use as Scratch
R0	A1	Argument / result /scratch register 1	Yes - Do not need to preserve original contents
R1	A2	Argument / result /scratch register 2	
R2	A3	Argument / scratch register 3	
R3	A4	Argument / scratch register 4	
R4	V1	Variable register 1	Yes - Must preserve original contents
R5	V2	Variable register 2	
R6	V3	Variable register 3	
R7	V4	Variable register 4	
R8	V5	Variable register 5	
R9	V6	Variable register 6	
R10	V7	Variable register 7	
R11	V8	Variable register 8	
R12	IP	Intra-Procedure-call scratch register	Do not use
R13	SP	Stack Pointer	
R14	LR	Link Register	
R15	PC	Program Counter	

3.5 FUNCTION CODING CONVENTIONS

Things can become a bit more complex when writing a function that calls another function if both functions have parameters. The challenge is that all functions must use the same registers (R0-R3) for their parameters, further complicated by the fact that these same registers are the ones whose content may be destroyed by calling another function.

Suppose you are writing function f1 in assembly and it calls function f2. The problem is that f2 may destroy the content of R0 through R3, where f1 is keeping its parameters. The solution is for function f1 to copy its parameters into R4 through R7 and to use only these registers for access to its parameters. That accomplishes two things: (1) these registers will not be modified by function f2 so that f1's parameters will still be available after a call to f2, and (2) it makes registers R0 through R3 available to pass parameters to function f2. Of course any register R4 through R7 used in this way must be preserved on entry and restored at exit by function f1.

Figure 3-10 illustrates this solution although introducing three new, but rather simple, instructions. The MOV instruction simply copies the content of R0 into R4, the LDR instruction loads the constant 4 into R0, and the ADD instruction replaces the content of R0 with the sum of R0 and R4. These instructions will be covered in greater detail later.

C Version	Assembly Version	

`int32_t f1(int32_t x)`
`{`
`    return f2(4) + x ;`
`}`
	`f1:  PUSH {R4,LR}`
	`      MOV  R4,R0`
	`      LDR  R0,=4`
	`      BL   f2`
	`      ADD  R0,R0,R4`
	`      POP  {R4,LR}`
	`      BX   LR`
		`// Preserve R4`
		`// Keep x safe in R4`
		`// R0 <-- f2's arg`
		`// R0 <-- f2(4)`
		`// R0 <-- f2(4) + x`
		`// Restore R4`
		`// Return result`

Figure 3-10 Two functions with parameters, one calling the other.

3.6 A COMPLETE EXAMPLE PROGRAM

To compile the programs in this book, you will need a computer with Windows 7 or higher and the following free software packages that may be downloaded by opening the following URL in a browser: http://www.engr.scu.edu/~dlewis/book3/

1. **EmBitz_0.42.zip**: The EmBitz C/C++ Integrated Development Environment (must be unzipped and installed)

2. **stsw-link004.zip**: The STM32 ST-LINK Utility from STMicroelectronics (must be unzipped and installed)

3. **EmBitzWorkspace.zip**: The preconfigured sample program project, workspace, include files and a runtime library compiled from a modified version of the STM32CubeF4 library available from STMicroelectronics.

4. **STM32F429I-DISCOVERY_Demo_V1.0.1.zip** (optional): Use this file and the ST-LINK utility to restore the original demo software that comes with the Discovery board.

Listing 3-1 is a complete example of a simple program written for the 32F429I-DISCO Discovery board. The source code is a project called "Sample_Program" within the EmBitz workspace. The main program calls an assembly language function that simply returns the sum of its integer argument and the constant one.

Every programming project created in EmBitz must specify a number of specific "Project Build Options". For those interested, the configuration process is described in the appendix. To make things easier, however, a pre-configured version of the program in Listing 3-1 has been provided. All you must do is start EmBitz, click on **File** and then **Open ...** and select **EmBitz workspace files** in the drop-down menu at the bottom of the dialog box. Navigate to the EmBitzWorkspace folder that contains the software from this book, select the file 32F429I-DISCO.eworkspace, and click on the **Open** button.

Main Program written in C

```c
#include <stdio.h>
#include <stdint.h>
#include "library.h"

extern uint32_t Add1(uint32_t x) ;

int main(void)
    {
    uint32_t strt, stop, before, after ;

    InitializeHardware(HEADER, PROJECT_NAME) ;

    before = 0 ;
    while (1)  // Never exit
        {
        strt  = GetClockCycleCount() ;
        after = Add1(before) ;
        stop  = GetClockCycleCount() ;

        printf("Before = %u\n", (unsigned) before) ;
        printf(" After = %u\n", (unsigned) after) ;
        printf("CPU Clock Cycles: %u\n", (unsigned) (stop - strt)) ;

        WaitForPushButton() ;
        ClearDisplay() ;
        before = after ;
        }
    }
```

Function written in Assembly

```asm
        .syntax    unified
        .cpu       cortex-m4
        .text
        .thumb_func
        .align    2

// uint32_t  Add1(uint32_t  x) ;

        .global    Add1
Add1:   ADD        R0,R0,1               // Return x + 1
        BX         LR

        .end
```

Listing 3-1 A complete C program and its assembly language function.

To compile the program:

1. Find the project name in the Management panel on the left side of the screen. Make sure that the name Sample_Program is in boldface, which indicates that the project is Active. If not, right-click on it and select **Activate project**.

2. Expand the project by clicking on the "+" sign immediately to the left of its name. Do the same for any subgroups found within it.

3. Double click on both main.c and Add1Function.s to view both files.

4. To compile the program, right-click on the project name and select **Build**. If there are any error or warning messages displayed, correct the source code of the function and recompile.

> *Hint: Function key **F7** is a short-cut for Build for the Active project.*

To download the program to the board and run it:

5. Connect the STM32F4 Discovery board to a USB port on your computer. This provides both power and a download connection to the device. To download the program to the board, click on **Debug > Start/stop Debug Session**.

> *Hint: Function key **F8** is a short-cut for Debug > Start/stop Debug Session.*

6. To run the program, click on **Debug > Run**. When the program begins to run it will display the first test case and pause. Press the left (blue) button to sequence through additional test cases. Verify that your program behaves as expected.

7. To end the debug session, click on **Debug > Start/stop Debug Session** again.

To create a Project Template using the current program with its entire preconfigured Project Build Options:

8. Click on **File > Save project as template ...**
    A dialog box will open. Enter a template name such as "STM32F429I-Discovery Template" and click on **OK**.

To create a new program, use the template to copy the same Project Build Options:

9. Click on **File > New > From template...**
    A dialog box will open. Click on the desired project template name and then click on **Go**.

10. A dialog box will open. Navigate to the folder named **EmBitzWorkspace**. In the same dialog box, click on **Make New Folder**. Enter a name for your new project and click **OK**.

11. A dialog box named "Change project's filename" will open. Enter the same name that you entered in the previous step and click on **OK**. A new project will be created in your workspace that contains a copy of the main.c and Add1Function.s files from the Sample Program. Edit these as desired, compile and download!

3.7 CUSTOM LIBRARY FUNCTIONS

In addition to the normal C library functions, the programs and assignments used in this book depend on a custom software library written for the STMicroelectronics 32F429I-DISCO Discovery kit. All of the functions in the library are intended to be called from a main program written in C. The library consists of a library archive file (library.a) that must be provided to the linker and an associated header file (library.h) that must be included in every C source code file. Other library functions and include files for using graphics and the touch screen are described in the Appendices.

3.7.1 Function InitializeHardware

Function prototype:

> void InitializeHardware(char *header, char *footer)

This function must be called as the first executable statement in the main program. It provides several initialization functions:

- Hardware: Initializes the processor, the CPU clock cycle counter, the display and the user push button.

- C Run-Time Environment: Creates a stack and heap in memory and provides initial values for all static variables.

- Display: Formats the display area, writing a text header at the top of the display, a text footer at the bottom, and configures the rest as a scrollable text area for use with printf.

3.7.2 Function WaitForPushButton

Function prototype:

> void WaitForPushButton(void)

This function causes the program to pause and wait for the user to push the blue user push button on the board.

3.7.3 Function PrintByte

Function prototype:

> void PrintByte(uint8_t byte)

This function displays a byte as a sequence of eight binary digits.

3.7.4 Function ClearDisplay

Function prototype:

> void ClearDisplay(void)

This function erases the scrollable area of the display. It does not erase either the header or the footer.

3.7.5 Function ClearGetClockCycleCount

Function prototype:

> uint32_t GetClockCycleCount(void)

This function returns the number of processor clock cycles since initialization. It is used to measure the relative execution time of code segments, and is useful for measuring the relative performance of various implementations of an assembly language function.

3.8 FUNCTION CALL AND RETURN INSTRUCTIONS

Table 3-2 is a summary of the basic instructions needed to call and return from functions. The register list of the PUSH and POP instructions are list of register names separated by commas or hyphens and enclosed in curly braces. Any subset of the register list may be replaced by a range specification, as in R0-R7. The stack uses the Stack Pointer (SP) to keep track of the current "top" of the stack. The stack is a descending stack, meaning that each register that is pushed causes SP to be decremented (by 4) first and then used to provide the address where the register is copied into memory. The register list for PUSH may include any registers except SP or PC. The register list for POP may not include SP; it may also not include PC if it contains LR, otherwise it may contain any other registers.

Table 3-2 ARM Cortex-M4 instructions used to call and return from functions.

Instruction	Format	Operation
Branch with Link	BL *label*	LR ← return address, PC ← address of label
Branch Indirect	BX R_m	PC ← R_m
Push registers onto stack	PUSH *register list*	SP ← SP − 4 × #registers Copy registers to mem[SP]
Pop registers from stack	POP *register list*	Copy mem[SP] to registers, SP ← SP + 4 × #registers

PROBLEMS

1. Translate each of the following C function calls into a sequence of ARM Cortex-M4 Instructions. Assume that all constants and variables are of type int32_t.
    (a) f1(a) ;
    (b) f2(&a) ;
    (c) f3(a, b) ;
    (d) b = f4() ;

2. Translate each of the following C function calls into a sequence of ARM Cortex-M4 Instructions. Assume that all constants and variables are of type uint64_t.
    (a) g1(a) ;
    (b) g2(&a) ;
    (c) g3(a, b) ;
    (d) b = g4() ;

3. Translate each of the following C function calls into a
    sequence of ARM Cortex-M4 Instructions. Assume
    that all constants and variables are of type int8_t.
    (a) h1(a) ;
    (b) h2(&a) ;
    (c) h3(a, b) ;
    (d) b = h4() ;

4. Translate each of the following functions into ARM
    Cortex-M4 assembly language:

    (a) uint64_t f4(uint32_t u32)
        {
        return (uint64_t) u32 ;
        }

    (b) int32_t f5(int32_t a, int32_t b)
        {
        // Prototype declaration
        int32_t f6(int32_t) ;

        return f6(a) + f6(b) ;
        }

    (c) uint32_t f7(uint32_t a, uint32_t b)
        {
        // Prototype declaration
        Uint32_t f8(uint32_t, uint32_t) ;

        return f8(b, a) ;
        }

(d) int32_t f9(int32_t a)
```
{
// Prototype declaration
int8_t f10(int8_t) ;

return a + (int32_t) f10(0) ;
}
```

(e) uint64_t f11(uint32_t a)
```
{
// Prototype declaration
uint32_t f12(uint32_t) ;

return (uint64_t) f12(a + 10) ;
}
```

PROGRAMMING PROBLEMS

5. Write an ARM Cortex-M4 assembly language function called "PrintTwo" that contains two calls to the C library function printf. The first call should display the value of an integer provided as the second parameter using a format specified by the first parameter. The second call to printf should display the value of numb + 1 on a second line. Note that there is only one call to function PrintTwo. Write a C program to test your function. The function prototype is:

```
void PrintTwo(char *format, int32_t numb) ;
```

CHAPTER 4
COPYING DATA

We obviously can't do much without data – whether it is in the form of constants or variables. The ARM processor uses what's known as a "Load/Store Architecture". That means that the only instructions that can access data that resides in memory are those that do nothing more than transfer data between memory and registers. More importantly, it also means that all *other* instructions – for example, those that perform arithmetic or logical operations - require that their operands and results be held in registers. Therefore we will need instructions to load constants into registers, instructions to load (copy) variables from memory into registers, and instructions to store the content of registers into variables that reside in memory.

4.1 COPYING CONSTANTS INTO REGISTERS

There are three instructions that can copy a constant into a register. The MOV instruction can be used to copy a small positive constant into a register, limited to unsigned 8-bit values and a few other "special" values.

```
MOV   R0,15  // Copies 15 into register R0
```

The MVN instruction copies the bitwise inverse of its operand into a register, and is also limited to unsigned 8-bit values and a few other "special" values.

```
MVN   R0,15  // Copies ~15 (same as -16) into R0
```

Since the bitwise inverse of a number is the one less than the negative of that number, the MVN instruction can effectively be used to copy small negative constants into a register. However, rather than require the programmer to remember how to use MVN to copy a negative constant, the assembler will automatically replace a MOV instruction that uses a negative constant into the equivalent MVN instruction.

```
MOV  R0,-16 // Assembler replaces with MVN R0,15
```

Larger constants can only be copied into a register by assigning a 32-bit memory location to hold the constant and using a regular LDR instruction to copy the constant from memory into a register. But rather than worry about which instruction to use, the assembler provides a "pseudo instruction" that makes the appropriate choice automatically, regardless of the actual value of the constant. Although it looks like a regular LDR instruction, the pseudo instruction is easily recognized because it is the only situation in which an equals sign (=) appears in the operand field:

```
LDR    R0,=12345 // Loads R0 with constant 12345
```

4.2 COPYING DATA FROM MEMORY TO REGISTERS

The LDR (Load Register) instruction copies the content of a 32-bit variable from its location in memory to a register. It's important to understand that the variable still resides in memory. Subsequent modification of the value in the register only affects the copy and has no effect on the value of the variable stored in memory.

```
LDR R0,word32    // Copies the value
                 // held in the 32-bit
                 // memory location
                 // labeled "word32"
                 // into register R0.
```

The LDRD (Load Register with Double) instruction is used to copy the content of a 64-bit variable into a pair of 32-bit registers:

```
LDRD R0,R1,dword64   // Copies the lower
                     // half of the value
                     // held in the 64-bit
                     // memory location
                     // labeled "dword64"
                     // into register R0,
                     // and the upper half
                     // into R1.
```

All of the processor registers hold exactly 32 bits, so when copying the content of an 8 or 16-bit memory location into a register, we must specify how to fill the extra bit positions in the register in a manner that provides the numerically equivalent 32-bit representation of the value.

4.2.1 Zero-Extending 8 and 16-bit Unsigned Integers

In order to preserve the numerical interpretation of an 8 or 16-bit unsigned value when promoting it to a 32-bit representation, the original operand must be right-justified within the destination and the extra bit positions must be filled with zeroes. This is what the LDRB (Load Byte) and LDRH (Load Half-word) instructions do:

```
LDRB  R0,ubyte8  // Copies the unsigned
                 // value held in the
                 // 8-bit memory location
                 // labeled "ubyte8" into
                 // bits 0-7 of register
                 // R0 and 0's into bits
                 // 8-31.
```

24 zeroes	ubyte8

⬇

register R0

```
LDRH  R0,uhalf16  // Copies the unsigned
                  // value held in the
                  // 16-bit memory location
                  // labeled "uhalf16" into
                  // bits 0-15 of register
                  // R0 and 0's into bits
                  // 16-31.
```

16 zeroes	uhalf16

⬇

register R0

4.2.2 Zero-Extending 32-Bit Unsigned Values to 64-Bits

To promote a 32-bit unsigned value from a single 32-bit register to a 64-bit register pair, we simply choose a register to hold the upper 32 bits and fill it with zeroes.

```
LDR  R0,uword32   // Copy "uword32" into R0
LDR  R1,=0        // Promote to 64-bits in R1.R0
```

4.2.3 Sign-Extending 8 and 16-Bit 2's Complement Integers

In order to preserve the numerical interpretation of an 8 or 16-bit signed 2's complement value when promoting it to a 32-bit representation, the original operand must be right-justified within the destination and the extra bit positions must be filled with copies of the sign bit (the most-significant bit of the operand). This is what the LDRSB (Load Signed Byte) and LDRSH (Load Signed Halfword) instructions do:

```
LDRSB R0,sbyte8  // Copies the signed
                 // value held in the
                 // 8-bit memory location
                 // labeled "sbyte8"
                 // into bits 0-7 of
                 // register R0 and 24
                 // copies of bit 7 of
                 // sbyte8 into bits 8-31.
```

```
LDRSH R0,shalf16 // Copies the signed
                 // value held in the
                 // 16-bit memory
                 // location labeled
                 // "shalf16" into bits
                 // 0-15 of R0 and 16
                 // copies of bit 15 of
                 // shalf16 into bits
                 // 16-31.
```

4.2.4 Sign-Extending 32-Bit 2's Complement Integers to 64-Bits

To promote a 32-bit signed value held in a register into a 64-bit register pair, we simply choose a register to hold the upper 32 bits, and use an ASR (Arithmetic Shift Right) instruction to fill it with copies of the sign bit. In the example, the ASR instruction copies the content of register R0 and shifts it right by one bit 31 times before storing the result in register R1. During each one-bit shift, bits 0 through 30 are each replaced by the value of the bit on their immediate left; bit 31 is unchanged. Repeating this 31 times causes all bits to become copies of bit 31. The result is then stored in register R1, which will contain all 0's if the value in R0 was positive, or all 1's if it was negative.

```
LDR R0,sword32   // Copy 32-bit "sword32" into R0
ASR R1,R0,31     // Promote to 64-bits in R1.R0
```

4.3 COPYING DATA FROM ONE REGISTER TO ANOTHER

Occasionally we will need to move a value from one register to another. This is done easily with the MOV instruction. Its first operand is the destination register and the second is the source register.

```
MOV R0,R1        // Copy from R1 to register R0
```

Note that the MOV instruction doesn't actually *move* the data; to do so would imply that that it would leave the source register empty. Instead, the MOV instruction simply makes a copy of the data in the source register and places that copy in the destination register.

4.4 COPYING DATA FROM REGISTERS TO MEMORY

The STR (Store Register) instruction copies the content of a register into a 32-bit variable located in memory. The instruction does not modify the content of the register.

```
STR   R0,word32  // Copies all 32 bits
                 // of the value held
                 // in register R0 into
                 // the 32-bit memory
                 // location labeled
                 // "word32".
```

The STRD (Store Register to Double) instruction copies the content of a pair of registers into a 64-bit variable located in memory. The instruction does not modify the content of either register.

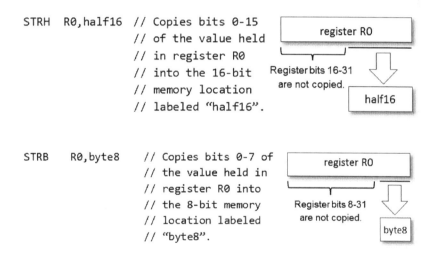

```
STRD R0,R1,dword64   // Copies the contents
                     // of register R0 into
                     // the lower half, and
                     // register R1 into the
                     // upper half, of the
                     // 64-bit memory location
                     // labeled "dword64".
```

register R1

register R0

dword64 (bits 32-63)

dword64 (bits 0-31)

When the destination variable in memory is only 8 or 16-bits wide, we use the STRB (Store Byte) and STRH (Store Half-word) instructions to copy the least-significant bits of a register into the variable. Like the regular STR, these instructions do not modify the content of the register.

```
STRH  R0,half16   // Copies bits 0-15
                  // of the value held
                  // in register R0
                  // into the 16-bit
                  // memory location
                  // labeled "half16".
```

register R0

Register bits 16-31 are not copied.

half16

```
STRB  R0,byte8   // Copies bits 0-7 of
                 // the value held in
                 // register R0 into
                 // the 8-bit memory
                 // location labeled
                 // "byte8".
```

register R0

Register bits 8-31 are not copied.

byte8

4.5 EXAMPLES OF COPYING DATA

Table 6-3 gives a number of examples that cover copying data from a source to a destination for all combinations of 8, 16, 32 and 64-bit signed and unsigned operands. A few of the entries in the table must be modified (as indicated by the footnotes) for cases involving the promotion of signed data types; all other entries will work for either signed or unsigned.

Table 4-1 Examples of copying 8, 16, 32 and 64-bit data.

Source	8-bit destination		16-bit destination		32-bit destination		64-bit destination	
Constant	LDR	R0,=5	LDR	R0,=5	LDR	R0,=5	LDR	R0,=5
	STRB	R0,dst8	STRH	R0,dst16	STR	R0,dst32	LDR[1]	R1,=0
							STRD	R0,R1,dst64
8-bit Variable	LDRB	R0,src8	LDRB[2]	R0,src8	LDRB[2]	R0,src8	LDRB[2]	R0,src8
	STRB	R0,dst8	STRH	R0,dst16	STR	R0,dst32	LDR[3]	R1,=0
							STRD	R0,R1,dst64
16-bit Variable	LDRB	R0,src16	LDRH	R0,src16	LDRH[4]	R0,src16	LDRH[4]	R0,src16
	STRB	R0,dst8	STRH	R0,dst16	STR	R0,dst32	LDR[3]	R1,=0
							STRD	R0,R1,dst64
32-bit Variable	LDRB	R0,src32	LDRH	R0,src32	LDR	R0,src32	LDR	R0,src32
	STRB	R0,dst8	STRH	R0,dst16	STR	R0,dst32	LDR[3]	R1,=0
							STRD	R0,R1,dst64
64-bit Variable	LDRB	R0,src64	LDRH	R0,src64	LDR	R0,src64	LDRD	R0,R1,src64
	STRB	R0,dst8	STRH	R0,dst16	STR	R0,dst32	STRD	R0,R1,dst64

[1] Replace with LDR R1,=-1 if source operand is a negative constant.
[2] Replace with LDRSB if source operand is signed.
[3] Replace with ASR R1,R0,31 if source operand is signed.
[4] Replace with LDRSH if source operand is signed.

4.6 ADDRESSING MODES

There isn't room in the binary representation of an instruction to include the full 32-bit address of a memory operand. Instead, operand addresses are computed using the contents of one or more registers and small constants called *displacements*. Instead of the actual operand address, what's stored in the instruction is a coded representation of how the address is to be calculated, which registers are involved, and the displacement constant (if any).

Table 4-2 The Offset Addressing Modes of the ARM Cortex-M4 Instruction Set

Name	Syntax	Address	Examples
Immediate Offset	[R_n{,constant}]	R_n + constant	1. [R5,100] 2. [R5]
Register Offset	[R_n,R_m{,LSL constant}]	R_n + (R_m << constant)	1. [R4,R5,LSL 2] 2. [R4,R5]

Table 4-2 lists the two primary addressing modes that the
ARM processor can use to calculate an operand address.

Immediate Offset mode uses the sum of a register and an optional constant as the operand address. The constant may be
positive or negative. If the value of the constant is zero, it may
be omitted as shown in the second example. The register is not
modified. Immediate Offset mode is useful when dereferencing a pointer; a previous instruction copies the pointer into a
register and then the register is used to provide the address.

Register Offset mode uses the sum of two registers as the operand address. The second register may be left-shifted by a
constant number of bit positions to effectively multiply it by a
power or two. If the shift constant is zero, the LSL option may
be omitted. Neither register is modified. Register Offset mode
is useful when subscripting an array; previous instructions
copy the starting address into the first register and the subscript
into the second. A shift option is used when the member elements of the array are 16, 32, or 64-bit values.

PC-Relative addressing is a special case of Immediate Offset
mode in which the register used to calculate the address is the
program counter (PC). During the execution of an instruction,
the program counter contains the address of the location immediately following the instruction. The location of an instruction that makes a direct reference to a variable by name is often
near the location of the variable. Thus the difference between
the program counter and the operand address is often a small
constant that can be represented with far fewer bits than a full
32-bit address. If the constant is between -255 and +4095[11],
the assembler will store it within the representation of the instruction. At run-time, the processor adds this displacement

---

[11] The LDRD instruction limits the range of displacements to ± 1020.

and the current value of the program counter to obtain the address of the operand.

Pre-Indexed and Post-Indexed addressing are similar to Immediate Offset addressing mode, but they also automatically update the value held in register R_n. The difference between the two is that Pre-Indexed addressing uses the updated value of the register and Post-Indexed uses the value prior to the update. These modes are useful in loops that process the elements of an array. First, register R_n would be initialized with the address of the first element of the array. Then during each iteration of the loop, pre- or post-indexing is used to access the array element *and* to automatically update the address in R_n to that of the next element in the array, eliminating the need for a separate instruction inside the loop to update the address.

Table 4-3 Pre- and Post-Indexed Addressing Modes of the ARM Cortex-M4 Instruction Set.

Name	Syntax	Address	Example	Left in R_n
Pre-Indexed	[R_n,constant]!	R_n+ constant	[R5,2]!	R_n+ constant
Post-Indexed	[R_n],constant	R_n	[R4],2	

The four options listed in Table 4-2 (Immediate Offset and Register Offset) and Table 4-3 (Pre-Indexed and Post-Indexed) are the only ways you are allowed to specify the address of an operand in memory. This includes PC-relative addressing, which may also be written as the name of a variable ± a constant. Common mistakes include using a subscripted array reference as in LDR R0,data[k], or using a variable name or an arithmetic operator inside the square brackets, as in LDR R0,[R0+k]

Figure 4-1 illustrates how the registers, a shifter, and a small constant are combined to generate the address of an instruction operand.

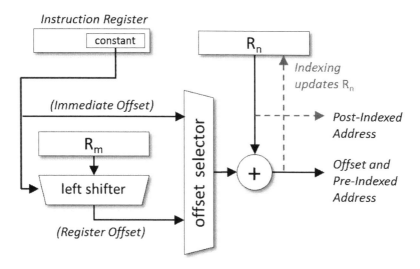

Figure 4-1 Conceptual model of ARM Address Calculation

4.7 POINTERS AND ARRAYS

The C "address of" operator (&)is often used to provide a value to be stored in a pointer. Since pointers hold an address, they are always 32 bits wide regardless of the size of the data stored at that address. The ARM assembly language equivalent of the address-of operator is the ADR (Address to Register) instruction. Although the operands of an ADR instruction include a register and a memory reference similar to an LDR instruction, there is no memory read as in the LDR. The ADR doesn't actually access the content of memory - it merely provides the address of its operand *without* causing a memory read or memory write.

Function call in C	Code produced by the compiler

`void f1(int32_t *) ;`
 	
`int32_t s32 ;`
`    .`
`    .`
`    f1(&s32) ;`
`    .`
`    .`
`    .`
	`    .`
	`    .`
	`    .`
	`ADR  R0,s32 // load R0 with &s32`
	`BL   f1      // call function f1`
	`    .`
	`    .`
	`    .`

Figure 4-2 Passing the address of a variable as a function parameter

Now let's see how a function might use this pointer in assembly. Assume that we would like to implement function f1 in assembly so that it behaves like the C function shown on the left side of Figure 4-3. The assignment statement stores the constant zero at an address that's held in the parameter p32 (a pointer). When function f1 was called earlier in Figure 4-2, the address of "s32" was copied into register R0 so that it could be provided as the value of the function's only parameter. Inside the C version of the function shown below, that value is referred to by the formal parameter "p32". However, that identifier is undefined inside the assembly language version of the function. Instead, the value of the formal parameter must be referred to by referencing the content of register R0.

Function in C	Function in assembly

`void f1(int32_t *p32)`
`{`
`    *p32 = 0 ;`
`}`
	`f1:  LDR R1,=0   // copy constant 0 into R1`
	`     STR R1,[R0] // store 0 at address in R0`
	`     BX  LR      // return`

Figure 4-3 A function dereferencing a pointer

The name of an array without a subscript is equivalent to the address of its first element and can be used as the parameter of f1. Calling f1 with the name of an array would generate a similar sequence of assembly language instructions:

Function call in C	Function call in assembly

`int32_t a32[100] ;`
 	
.
.
.
`f1(a32) ;`
.
.
.
	.
	.
	.
	`ADR  R0,a32  // load R0 with &a32[0]`
	`BL   f1       // call function f1`
	.
	.
	.

Figure 4-4 Using the name of an array to pass its address to a function

It's also important to understand how pointer arithmetic works. Let's modify f1 so that it adds 1 to the pointer before storing the zero so that when the parameter is the array a32, it stores zero into the second element of the array (a32[1]). Note than in the assembly version of the function shown below, we add 4 (not 1) to the pointer because each element of the array contains four bytes at four consecutive addresses. I.e., if a32[0] is at address 1000, then a32[1] is at address 1004, etc.

Function in C	Function in assembly

`void f1(int32_t *p32)`
`{`
`    *(p32 + 1) = 0 ;`
`}`
	`f1: LDR  R1,=0      // copy constant 0 into R1`
	`    STR  R1,[R0,4] // address given by R0 + 4`
	`    BX   LR         // return`

Figure 4-5 A function dereferencing a pointer expression

Now consider a different function f2 with two parameters – the first declared to be an array and the second declared to be an integer. We've seen how using the name of an array without a subscript is equivalent to a constant pointer whose value is the address of the first element in the array. Therefore it should come as no surprise that declaring a parameter as an array is no different than declaring it as a pointer to data of the same type.

Function in C	Function in assembly
| ```
void f2(int32_t a32[], int32_t k32)
  {
  a32[k32] = 0 ;
  }
``` | ```
f2:  LDR   R2,=0
     STR   R2,[R0,R1,LSL 2]
     BX    LR
``` |

Figure 4-6 A function making a subscripted array reference

The only real difference between the assembly code in Figure 4-5 and that of Figure 4-6 is that we add a variable (the subscript) instead of a constant to the address. As before, we still have to multiply by 4 before the addition. E.g., in Figure 4-5, the constant 1 became 4 when translated to assembly; in Figure 4-6, the subscript variable k32 is multiplied by 4 by shifting it left two bits. Using a left-shift to perform the multiplication is particularly useful because we normally work with data that is 1, 2, 4 or 8 bytes in width.

Another interesting property of pointer arithmetic is that the difference of two pointers is not merely the numerical difference between the two address values they contain. For example, consider two pointers p1 and p2 that are both pointers to data of type int32_t. Assume that p1 contains the address 1000_{10}. From pointer arithmetic, we know that the assignment statement,

```
p2 = p1 + 1 ;
```

stores the value 1004_{10} into p2. But this assignment statement also implies that the difference p2 − p1 should be 1, not 4. That means that the assembly code to implement p2 − p1 must be a subtraction followed by a division by 4, usually implemented using an arithmetic shift right (ASR) instruction.

4.8 POINTERS AND STRUCTURES

When an integer variable is given as a function parameter, C provides a copy of its contents to the function. However, when the name of an array is given as a function parameter, rather than making a copy of the contents of the array (which might take an excessive amount of run-time to create), C instead provides the function with the starting address of the array – i.e., a pointer to the first element in the array. Structs are generally smaller than arrays, so when a struct is used as a function parameter, C provides a copy. (Interestingly, you can put an array inside a struct and pass the struct to a function, thus forcing the compiler to provide a copy of the array.)

Arrays and structs are the two most frequently used examples of aggregate data types in C – that is, a type comprised of several different data items. When a function in assembly needs access to a struct, it's simplest to pass the address of the struct which also gives the function the option of modifying the data within the struct. However, how to determine the address of a member element within the struct requires a bit of explanation.

Consider the declaration of structure s shown in Figure 4-7. You might reasonably expect that the value of sizeof(s) to be 14, and that if the address of s is 1000_{16}, that the addresses of s.x32, s.y16, and s.z64 to be 1000_{16}, 1004_{16}, and 1006_{16} respectively. However, that would not be the case. As shown in the figure, 32-bit and 64-bit items are placed at addresses that are a multiple of four (i.e., a mod 4 address), and 16-bit items are placed at addresses that are a multiple of two (a mod 2 address). This is the default behavior of the compiler and is known as *structure padding*.

```
struct
   {
   uint32_t   x32 ; // 4 bytes
   uint16_t   y16 ; // 2 bytes
   uint64_t   z64 ; // 8 bytes
   } s ;
```

	Addresses
← 4 bytes (32 bits) →	
s.z64 (bits 63..32)	100C – 100F
s.z64 (bits 31..0)	1008 – 100B
not used s.y16	1004 – 1007
s.x32	1000 – 1003

Figure 4-7 Memory layout with default structure padding.

Logically, we picture memory as a collection of bytes, each with its own address, with larger items stored as a contiguous sequence of bytes. For performance, however, the *physical* implementation of memory is organized into words of four bytes each so that an 8-bit byte, a 16-bit halfword, or a 32-bit word can each be retrieved in a single memory access. For example, if structure padding is disabled to conserve memory as shown in Figure 4-8, it would take three memory read cycles instead of two to retrieve the 64-bit member s.z64.

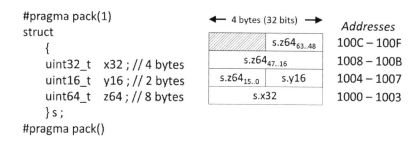

```
#pragma pack(1)
struct
   {
   uint32_t   x32 ; // 4 bytes
   uint16_t   y16 ; // 2 bytes
   uint64_t   z64 ; // 8 bytes
   } s ;
#pragma pack()
```

	Addresses
← 4 bytes (32 bits) →	
$s.z64_{63..48}$	100C – 100F
$s.z64_{47..16}$	1008 – 100B
$s.z64_{15..0}$ s.y16	1004 – 1007
s.x32	1000 – 1003

Figure 4-8 Memory layout with structure padding disabled.

The tradeoff between using default structure padding to improve run-time performance, or using packed structures to conserve memory has an obvious impact on the displacement constant needed in assembly to reference a member element of the structure as shown in Figure 4-9.

Function Call in C	Structure Padding Enabled	Structure Padding Disabled
f(&s) ;	f: // R0 = &s ... LDRD R1,R2,[R0,8] ... BX LR	f: // R0 = &s ... LDRD R1,R2,[R0,6] ... BX LR

Figure 4-9 Impact of structure padding on the displacement constant needed to access member element s.z64

4.9 COPYING A BLOCK OF DATA QUICKLY

Suppose you need to copy a large block of data, such as the contents of an array or memory buffer, and you need the code to execute as fast as possible. You could obviously write a loop to perform the copy, but a faster solution when the size of the block is a constant is to unroll the loop into a straight-line sequence of instructions. Fortunately, the ARM Cortex-M4 instruction set includes instructions that can copy several bytes of memory in one instruction.

The Load Multiple and Increment After (LDMIA) instruction copies data from memory into a list of registers. The instruction has two operands: The first operand is a register that provides the address; the register may be followed by an optional write-back flag (!) to specify that the register should be updated with the address following the data in memory. The second operand is a list of registers or register ranges, separated by commas and enclosed in curly braces. The order of the registers in the list is irrelevant – they are loaded from memory in *increasing* numerical order. Note that "LDMIA SP!,*register list*" is equivalent to "POP *register list*". The Store Multiple and Increment After (STMIA) instruction is similar to LDMIA except that STMIA copies *from* registers *to* memory.

```
// Copy data starting at mem[R0]
```

Last word	↑ Increasing
•••	addresses
2nd word	
RO → 1st word	

```
LDMIA R0,{R1,R2}   // regs ← mem
STMIA R0!,{R3-R5}  // regs → mem
```

Two similar instructions not used in Listing 4-1 are Load Multiple and Decrement Before (LDMDB) and Store Multiple and Decrement Before (STMDB). The Load Multiple and Decrement Before (LDMDB) instruction also copies data from memory into a list of registers. As before, the order of the registers in the list is irrelevant – but they are loaded from memory in *decreasing* numerical order. The Store Multiple and Decrement Before (STMDB) instruction is similar to LDMDB except that STMDB copies *from* registers *to* memory. Note that "STMDB SP!,*register list*" is equivalent to "PUSH *register list*".

```
// Copy data ending before mem[R0]   RO →
```

1st word	↑ Increasing
2nd word	addresses
•••	
Last word	

```
LDMDB R0,{R1,R2}   // regs <-- mem
STMDB R0!,{R3-R5}  // regs --> mem
```

```
        .syntax unified
        .cpu      cortex-m4
        .text
        .thumb_func
        .align    2

// void Copy512Bytes(void *dst, const void *src)

        .global  Copy512Bytes

Copy512Bytes:
        PUSH      {R4-R12}    // Preserve registers R4 - R12

// The ".rept 11" and ".endr" directives insert 11 copies
// of the LDMIA/STMIA instructions. Each pair copies 11
// words of 4 bytes (44 bytes) of data from the address in
// R1 to the address in R0, and updates those addresses by
// 44 in preparation for the next copy. This copies 484
// bytes, leaving 28 more to be copied.

        .rept     11
        LDMIA     R1!,{R2-R12}
        STMIA     R0!,{R2-R12}
        .endr

// Copy the remaining 7*4 = 28 bytes

        LDMIA     R1,{R2-R8}
        STMIA     R0,{R2-R8}

        POP       {R4-R12}    // Restore registers R4 - R12
        BX        LR          // Return

        .end
```

Listing 4-1 A fast assembly language function to copy a block of 512 bytes of data.

4.10 INSTRUCTIONS USED TO COPY DATA

Table 4-4 and Table 4-5 provide a summary of the instructions (in addition to PUSH and POP that were introduced in an earlier chapter) that may be used to copy data. Note: MOVS and MVNS affect flags N, Z and C.

Table 4-4 ARM Cortex-M4 instructions for copying to or from a single register.

Instruction	Syntax	Operation
Move	MOV{S} R_d,*Op2*	$R_d \leftarrow Op2$
Move NOT	MVN{S} R_d,*Op2*	$R_d \leftarrow \sim Op2$
Load PC-relative Address	ADR R_d,*label*	$R_d \leftarrow$ address of label
Load Register with word	LDR R_d,*mem32*	$R_d \leftarrow$ a 32-bit memory location
Load Register with Byte	LDRB R_d,*mem8*	$R_d \leftarrow$ (uint8_t) memory location
Load Register with Signed Byte	LDRSB R_d,*mem8*	$R_d \leftarrow$ (int8_t) memory location
Load Register with Halfword	LDRH R_d,*mem16*	$R_d \leftarrow$ (uint16_t) memory location
Load Register with Signed Halfword	LDRSH R_d,*mem16*	$R_d \leftarrow$ (int16_t) memory location
Store Register word	STR R_d,*mem32*	$R_d \rightarrow$ a 32-bit memory location
Store Register Byte	STRB R_d,*mem8*	$R_d \rightarrow$ an 8-bit memory location
Store Register Halfword	STRH R_d,*mem16*	$R_d \rightarrow$ an 16-bit memory location

Table 4-5 ARM Cortex-M4 instructions for copying to or from multiple registers.

Instruction	Syntax	Operation
Load Register with two words	LDRD $R_{dlo}, R_{dhi}, mem64$	$R_{dhi}, R_{dlo} \leftarrow$ 64-bit memory location
Load Multiple registers, Increment After[1]	LDMIA $R_n!, register\ list$	registers $\leftarrow$ memory, 1st address in R_n; Updates R_n only if write-back flag (!) is appended to R_n.
Load Multiple registers, Decrement Before	LDMDB $R_n!, register\ list$	registers $\leftarrow$ memory, addresses end just before address in R_n; Updates R_n only if write-back flag (!) is appended to R_n.
Store Register two words	STRD $R_{dlo}, R_{dhi}, mem64$	$R_{dhi}, R_{dlo} \rightarrow$ 64-bit memory location
Store Multiple registers, Increment After	STMIA $R_n!, register\ list$	registers $\rightarrow$ memory, 1st address in R_n; Updates R_n only if write-back flag (!) is appended to R_n.
Store Multiple registers, Decrement Before[2]	STMDB $R_n!, register\ list$	registers $\rightarrow$ memory, addresses end just before address in R_n; Updates R_n only if write-back flag (!) is appended to R_n.

[1] LDMIA SP!,{reglist} is equivalent to POP {reglist}.
[2] STMDB SP!{reglist} is equivalent to PUSH {reglist}.

PROBLEMS

1. For each of the following, give C declarations for each of the variables and C assignment statements which accomplish the same thing. Specify signed or unsigned wherever it can be determined; otherwise leave it off the declaration.

```
(a)   LDR      R0,green
      ADD      R0,R0,1
      LDR      R1,=0
      STRD     R0,R1,violet


(b)   LDRH     R0,red
      ADR      R1,blue
      LDR      R2,purple
      STRH     R0,[R1,R2,LSL 1]


(c)   LDR      R0,black
      LDRSB    R1,white
      ADD      R0,R0,R1,LSL 2
      LDR      R1,=0
      STR      R1,[R0]
```

2. Given the C declaration statements,

```
uint8_t   u8  ;
uint16_t  u16 ;
uint32_t  u32 ;
uint64_t  u64 ;
```

Translate each of the following C assignment statements into ARM Cortex-M4 assembly:

```
(a)   u8  = 0 ;          (g)   u32 = u16 ;
(b)   u16 = 0 ;          (h)   u64 = u32 ;
(c)   u32 = 0 ;          (i)   u8  = u32 ;
(d)   u64 = 0 ;          (j)   u8  = u16 ;
(e)   u16 = u8 ;         (k)   u16 = u32 ;
(f)   u32 = u8 ;
```

3. Given the C declaration statements,

```
int8_t    s8 ;
int16_t   s16 ;
int32_t   s32 ;
int64_t   s64 ;
```

Translate each of the following C assignment statements into ARM Cortex-M4 assembly:

```
(a)   s8  = -1 ;   (g)   s32 = s16 ;
(b)   s16 = -1 ;   (h)   s64 = s32 ;
(c)   s32 = -1 ;   (i)   s8  = s32 ;
(d)   s64 = -1 ;   (j)   s8  = s16 ;
(e)   s16 = s8 ;   (k)   s16 = s32 ;
(f)   s32 = s8 ;
```

4. Given the C declaration statements,

```
int8_t    s8, *ps8 ;
int32_t   s32, *ps32 ;
```

Translate each of the following C assignment statements into ARM Cortex-M4 assembly:

```
(a)   ps32 = &s32 ;
(b)   ps8 = &s8 ;
(c)   ps8++ ;
(d)   ps32++ ;
(e)   *ps32 = 0 ;
(f)   *(ps8 + 1) = 0 ;
(g)   *(ps32 + 1) = 0 ;
(h)   *(ps32 + s32) = 0 ;
(i)   ((int8_t *) &s32)[1] = 0 ;
```

5. Translate each of the following C assignment statements into ARM Cortex-M4 assembly:

    (a) `int64_t a64[10] ;`
        `int32_t k32, *p32 ;`

        `p32 = ((int32_t *) &a64[k32]) + 1 ;`

    (b) `int16_t **pp16 ;`

        `*(*pp16 + 1) = 0 ;`

    (c) `int32_t k32, a32[10], *p32 ;`

        `k32 = &a32[k32] - p32 ;`

    (d) `int16_t a16[10] ;`
        `int32_t k32 ;`

        `++a16[k32 - 1] ;`

    (e) `uint32_t u32 ;`
        `uint64_t u64 ;`

        `u64 = (uint64_t) u32 ;`

    (f) `int8_t s8 ;`
        `int64_t s64 ;`

        `s64 = (int64_t) s8 ;`

PROGRAMMING PROBLEMS

6. Write a function in ARM Cortex-M4 assembly to return a pointer to the item at row r, column c of a two-dimensional array of 32-bit integers stored in row major format. The array begins at the address held in pointer p and the number of items in each row is given by cols.

Write a C program to test your function. The function prototype is:

```
int32_t *pWord(int32_t *p, uint32_t cols,
        uint32_t r, uint32_t c) ;
```

7. Write a function in ARM Cortex-M4 assembly to swap the contents of its two actual arguments of type int32_t. Write a C program to test your function. The function prototype is:

```
void Swap32(int32_t *p1, int32_t *p2) ;
```

8. Write a function in ARM Cortex-M4 assembly to swap the contents of its two actual arguments of type int64_t. Write a C program to test your function. The function prototype is:

```
void Swap64(int64_t *p1, int64_t *p2) ;
```

9. Write a pair of functions in ARM Cortex-M4 assembly to simulate a stack. The data is held in a fixed-size array of 100 32-bit words. A pop returns the word at index position 0 and then shifts all remaining 99 words up; a push shifts the first 99 words down one position and then copies the new item into position 0. (Do not use a loop.) Write a C program to test your functions. The function prototypes are:

```
uint32_t Pop(uint32_t *pArray) ;

void Push(uint32_t *pArray, uint32_t item) ;
```

CHAPTER 5
INTEGER ARITHMETIC

Even the most primitive processor needs to be able to perform basic arithmetic. While our processor provides instructions for the four basic arithmetic operators, that's not always true of other processors. Multiplication and especially division are much more difficult to implement in hardware than addition and subtraction, so it's not uncommon to find that an inexpensive processor has no divide instruction, or maybe not even a multiply. Performing multiplication and division with these processors requires calling functions that implement iterative algorithms in assembly. Early versions of the ARM processor, for example, provided no divide instruction, and the first version even had no multiply. Even though the ARM Cortex-M4F processor used in this book provides both multiply and divide instructions, there are limitations to what they can do. For these reasons, we will explore efficient ways to do arithmetic in this and the following chapter.

5.1 CONDITION FLAGS

The result of a calculation has certain properties, such as the sign of the result, whether or not a carry, borrow or overflow occurred, and whether or not the result is zero. The ARM processor keeps this information as a set of one-bit "condition flags" in a special 32-bit Application Processor Status Register (APSR). These flags will be used in the following sections to make decisions and to implement multiple-precision shifts, addition and subtraction on operands larger than 32-bits.

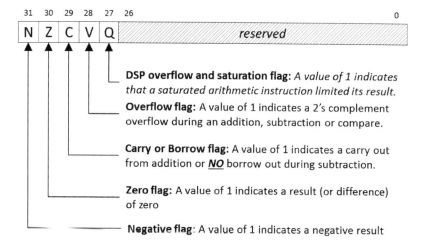

Figure 5-1 The ARM Application Processor Status Register

None of the data movement instructions (moves, loads, stores, pushes and pops) modify the flags. Many of the other instructions, however, may update the flags with the properties of their result - but only you append the letter 'S' to the end of the instruction mnemonic. The flags updated by an instruction when the 'S' is added appear in the last column of the tables that follow.

5.2 ADDITION AND SUBTRACTION

The ARM processor provides a large variety of instructions for addition and subtraction. However, most are rarely used; those used most frequently are summarized in Table 5-1.

The symbol "*Op2*" shown in the table represents a third operand that may be either a constant or a register[12]. For example,

```
ADD   R0,R0,5    // R0 is replaced by R0 + 5
ADD   R0,R1,R2   // R0 is replaced by R1 + R2
```

---

[12] Later we'll learn that *Op2* may also be a shifted copy of a register's contents.

Table 5-1 Basic ARM Cortex-M4 addition and subtraction instructions[13].

Instruction	Format	Operation	Flags
Add	ADD{S} Rd,Rn,Op2	Rd ← Rn + Op2	N,Z,C,V
Add with Carry	ADC{S} Rd,Rn,Op2	Rd ← Rn + Op2 + Carry	N,Z,C,V
Subtract	SUB{S} Rd,Rn,Op2	Rd ← Rn − Op2	N,Z,C,V
Subtract with Carry	SBC{S} Rd,Rn,Op2	Rd ← Rn − Op2 − ~Carry	N,Z,C,V
Reverse Subtract	RSB{S} Rd,Rn,Op2	Rd ← Op2 − Rn	N,Z,C,V

The instruction name "Subtract with Carry" may seem odd since we think of subtraction involving borrows, not carries. But ARM implements the subtraction A-B using the equivalent A+~B+1, which records a carry out of 0 when the borrow out would have been 1. This use of the carry flag as an "inverse" representation of the borrow also means that subtraction with borrow (A-B-borrow) is actually implemented as (A+~B+carry). If this is confusing, just think of SBC as "Subtract with Borrow".

The Reverse Subtract (RSB) instruction is provided because Op2 makes it easier to compute the difference of a constant less a register. A pseudo instruction named "NEG" takes advantage of this to create what appears to be an instruction to copy the negative of one register to another, as in:

```
NEG R0,R1  // Replaced by RSB R0,R1,0
```

5.2.1 Carries and Overflow

The N-bit result produced by the addition of two N-bit numbers is the same whether the operands are signed or unsigned,

---

[13] The processor provides several other rarely-used addition and subtraction instructions not listed in this table.

so there is only one ADD instruction for both types of data. When you add two unsigned N-bit numbers, a carry out of 1 occurs when the sum is too large to fit within N bits and indicates that an overflow has occurred – meaning that the result is outside the range of values that can be represented as an N-bit unsigned number. For 2's complement however, a carry out of 1 does *not* necessarily indicate an overflow. For example, adding two negative values *always* produces a carry out and adding two positive numbers *never* produces a carry out – regardless of whether an overflow occurs or not. For 2's complement, the hardware detects an overflow when the carry in and out of the most-significant bit position (the sign bit) are different.

What's important to understand here is that the values stored in the flags are determined by hardware that doesn't know if you're interpreting the operands as signed or unsigned. If the operands are unsigned, an overflow during addition is indicated by 1 in the carry flag (C), and by 0 during subtraction (same as a borrow out of 1). Conversely, if the operands are signed, an overflow is indicated by a 1 in the overflow flag (V) for either addition or subtraction. In either case, the flags are only updated if you appended an 'S' to the end of the instruction mnemonic.

5.2.2 Multiple Precision

Suppose we are writing a program that uses very large integers of 128 bits, each stored as an array of four 32-bit words. Since the ARM is a 32-bit processor, we must use a *"multiple precision"* sequence to add 32 bits at a time, propagating the carry from one addition to the next. Listing 5-1 is a function to add two such numbers. The function has three formal parameters: an array "sum" to hold the result, and arrays "num1" and "num2" to hold the two operands.

```
        .syntax     unified
                    .cpu        cortex-m4
        .text
        .thumb_func
        .align      2

// void Add128(int32_t sum[], int32_t num1[], int32_t num2[]) ;

        .global     Add128

Add128: PUSH        {R4-R6}         // Preserve R4, R5, R6
        LDRD        R3,R4,[R1],8    // R4.R3 = num1 bits 63-0
        LDRD        R5,R6,[R2],8    // R6.R5 = num2 bits 63-0
        ADDS        R3,R3,R5        // R3 = sum bits 31-0
        ADCS        R4,R4,R6        // R4 = sum bits 63-32
        STRD        R3,R4,[R0],8    // Store sum bits 63-0
        LDRD        R3,R4,[R1]      // R4.R3 = num1 bits 127-64
        LDRD        R5,R6,[R2]      // R6.R5 = num2 bits 127-64
        ADCS        R3,R3,R5        // R3 = sum bits 95-64
        ADC         R4,R4,R6        // R4 = sum bits 127-96
        STRD        R3,R4,[R0]      // Store sum bits 127-64
        POP         {R4-R6}         // Restore R4, R5, R6
        BX          LR              // Return

        .end
```

Listing 5-1 Assembly language function to add two 128-bit integers.

The function requires the use of seven registers; functions are allowed to modify R0 through R3, but R4, R5 and R6 must be pushed onto the stack to preserve their original content. The code captures the carry out of each addition in the carry flag by appending the letter 'S' to the add instructions, and includes the carry in the next addition with ADC instructions. To minimize the number of instructions, the function uses LDRD and STRD to copy 64 bits (8 bytes) at a time, with post-indexed addressing to automatically advance the addresses of their 64-bit operands.

5.3 MULTIPLICATION

As was the case for addition and subtraction, the ARM Cortex-M4F processor provides a large variety of multiply instructions. However, most are rarely used; those used most frequently are summarized in Table 5-2.

Table 5-2 Basic ARM Cortex-M4 multiply instructions[14].

Instruction	Format	Operation
32-bit Multiply	MUL{S} R_d, R_n, R_m	$R_d \leftarrow$ (int32_t) $R_n \times R_m$
32-bit Multiply with Accumulate	MLA R_d, R_n, R_m, R_a	$R_d \leftarrow R_a +$ (int32_t) $R_n \times R_m$
32-bit Multiply & Subtract	MLS R_d, R_n, R_m, R_a	$R_d \leftarrow R_a -$ (int32_t) $R_n \times R_m$
64-bit Unsigned Multiply	UMULL $R_{dlo}, R_{dhi}, R_n, R_m$	$R_{dhi}R_{dlo} \leftarrow$ (uint64_t) $R_n \times R_m$
64-bit Unsigned Multiply with Accumulate	UMLAL $R_{dlo}, R_{dhi}, R_n, R_m$	$R_{dhi}R_{dlo} \leftarrow R_{dhi}R_{dlo} +$ (uint64_t) $R_n \times R_m$
64-bit Signed Multiply	SMULL $R_{dlo}, R_{dhi}, R_n, R_m$	$R_{dhi}R_{dlo} \leftarrow$ (int64_t) $R_n \times R_m$
64-bit Signed Multiply with Accumulate	SMLAL $R_{dlo}, R_{dhi}, R_n, R_m$	$R_{dhi}R_{dlo} \leftarrow R_{dhi}R_{dlo} +$ (int64_t) $R_n \times R_m$

MULS affects flags N and Z. No other multiply instruction affects the flags.

5.3.1 Signed versus Unsigned Products

When you do multiplication by hand using paper and pencil, the number of digits in the product can be as many as the sum of the number in the two operands. It's the same in binary. If we multiply two 4-bit numbers, there can be as many as eight bits in the product. Consider the product of two 4-bit operands, 1100_2 and 0110_2. If interpreted as unsigned integers, they are 12_{10} and 6_{10} whose product is 72_{10}, represented as the double-

---

[14] The processor provides several other rarely-used multiply instructions not listed in this table.

length product $0100\ 1000_2$. However, if interpreted as 2's complement integers, they are -4_{10} and $+6_{10}$ whose product is -24_{10}, represented as $1110\ 1000_2$.

Since the unsigned and 2'c complement products are different, most computers have two different multiply instructions – one for unsigned operands and another for 2's complement. But notice that the difference between the two products only occurs in the most-significant half of the double-length result. In fact, the least significant halves will always be the same and is important when you consider how multiplication works in a high-level language.

In C, the data type of an expression is determined by the data type of the operands. Therefore the product of two N-bit integers is also an N-bit integer. The code produced by the compiler only uses the least-significant half of the double-length product, so it doesn't matter whether the compiler uses a signed or an unsigned multiply instruction.

The MUL instruction of the ARM processor was intended for use by a compiler, and so it only produces a 32-bit product from 32-bit operands. If you need the full 64-bit product, you must use UMULL (unsigned) or SMULL (2's complement) instructions. The other multiply instructions in Table 5-2 are used in applications such as series approximations that involve computing the sum of a sequence of terms.

Unlike most of the other instructions for performing arithmetic, all of the multiply instructions require that all of their operands reside in registers. I.e., a multiply instruction can't specify a constant as an operand. The constant must first be copied into a register, and then use that register as one of the operands of the multiply.

There was a very simple function called Mult32x32 introduced at the beginning of this book as an example of what assembly language looks like. Although it only contained two instructions, calling it in C provides an efficient means to get the full 64-bit product of two 32-bit two's complement integers. That's important when evaluating an expression like a*b/c; the product may be too large to fit in the same number of bits as the operands, causing an incorrect result even when that final result would fit after the division. The only other way to get a 64-bit product from 32-bit operands in C requires promoting the operands to 64 bits before multiplying, as in:

$$((\text{int64\_t}) \ a) \ * \ ((\text{int64\_t}) \ b)$$

However, this means performing a 64×64 multiplication – something that requires calling a much slower run-time library function.

5.3.2 64x64 Single-Length Products

So how would you write a library function in ARM assembly to produce the single-length 64-bit product of two 64-bit numbers? Start by recognizing that if we split A and B into their respective 32-bit halves, we can write:

$$A \times B = \ (2^{32} A_{63..32} + A_{31..00}) \times (2^{32} B_{63..32} + B_{31..00})$$

Expanding the product yields:

$$A \times B = 2^{64} A_{63..32} B_{63..32} + 2^{32}(A_{63..32} B_{31..00} + A_{31..00} B_{63..32}) + A_{31..00} B_{31..00}$$

Since we only need a single-length (64-bit) product, we can discard the first term entirely. Moreover, since multiplying the two cross-products by 2^{32} is equivalent to shifting them left by 32 bits, we only need the least-significant half of their 64-bit products and can therefore use MLA to add their single-length

(32-bit) products to the result. The partial products are then combined as illustrated in Figure 5-2:

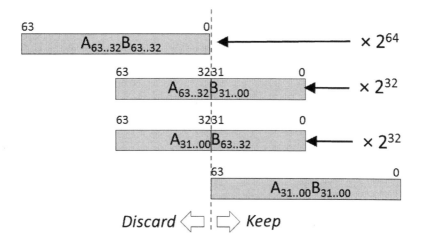

Figure 5-2 Implementing a single-length 64x64 product.

Now we can write the following very efficient function in
ARM assembly:

```
          .syntax unified
          .cpu    cortex-m4
          .text
          .thumb_func
          .align  2

 // Function prototype: int64_t Mult64x64(int64_t A, int64_t B) ;

          .global Mult64x64

Mult64x64: // R0 = bits A31..A00  (Alo)
           // R1 = bits A63..A32  (Ahi)
           // R2 = bits B31..B00  (Blo)
           // R3 = bits B63..B32  (Bhi)

           PUSH    {R4,R5}         // Preserve R4, R5
           UMULL   R4,R5,R0,R2     // R5.R4 = Alo x Blo
           MLA     R5,R1,R2,R5     // R5 = R5 + Ahi x Blo
           MLA     R1,R0,R3,R5     // R1 = R5 + Alo x Bhi
           MOV     R0,R4           // R0 = lower half of result
           POP     {R4,R5}         // Restore R4, R5
           BX      LR // Return

          .end
```

Listing 5-2 Assembly language function to multiply two 64-bit
integers

5.3.3 Multiplication Overflow

In multiplication, an overflow is impossible when using a double-length product. Thus a multiplication overflow is only defined as a result that exceeds the range of values permitted by a
single-length product.

For unsigned products, we say that a multiplication overflow
has occurred whenever the upper half of the double-length
product is non-zero. For 2's complement products, however, as
overflow occurs when the upper half is not a sign-extension of
the lower half. I.e., the upper half of a positive product must

be all 0's and the upper half of a negative product must be all 1's or else an overflow has occurred.

The ARM processor doesn't use the overflow flag (V) to indicate an overflow during multiplication. Whether the product is signed or unsigned, determining overflow requires checking the upper half of the double-length product. Since the MUL, MLA and MLS instructions only produce a single-length product, it's usually computationally impractical[15] to know when they have caused an overflow.

5.4 DIVISION

If you think of division as the inverse of multiplication, then you might expect the dividend to be a 64-bit double-length quantity. However, the instruction set was designed to be used in code generated by a compiler, so the only two divide instructions that are provided both use a 32-bit divisor and a 32-bit dividend to produce a 32-bit quotient. Neither affects the flags.

Table 5-3 The ARM Cortex-M4 divide instructions

Instruction	Format	Operation
Unsigned Divide	UDIV R_d,R_n,R_m	$R_d \leftarrow$ (uint32_t) $R_n \div R_m$
Signed Divide	SDIV R_d,R_n,R_m	$R_d \leftarrow$ (int32_t) $R_n \div R_m$

---

[15] A somewhat complex algorithm for determining overflow in a single-length multiplication appears in Warren, Henry S. *Hacker's Delight*. Upper Saddle River, NJ: Addison-Wesley, 2013.

5.4.1 Signed versus Unsigned

We saw earlier that one multiply instruction can be used for both unsigned and 2's complement single-length multiplication. That might lead you to expect that since the divide instructions use a single-length dividend, that one instruction could be used for either unsigned or 2's complement division. However, that's not true. For example, consider dividing the 8-bit number 11110000_2 by 4:

Unsigned			Signed		
11110000_2	=	240_{10}	11110000_2	=	-16_{10}
$240_{10} \div 4$	=	60_{10}	$-16_{10} \div 4$	=	-4_{10}
60_{10}	=	$\underline{00}111100_2$	-4_{10}	=	$\underline{11}111100_2$

Figure 5-3 Difference between signed and 2's complement division

5.4.2 Division Overflow

An overflow during division means that the quotient is too large to fit within its range of representation. When a double-length dividend is divided by a single-length divisor, overflow may occur whenever the magnitude of the dividend is much larger than that of the divisor. However, limiting the dividend to a single-length quantity significantly reduces its possible magnitude - so much so that overflow becomes impossible except in two cases: (1) when dividing by zero, or (2) when attempting a signed divide with a full-scale negative dividend and a divisor of -1. Note that neither of the ARM divide instructions modify the overflow flag (V); determining if an overflow occurs during division is left to the programmer.

5.4.3 Calculating a Remainder

There is no instruction in the ARM processor that calculates a remainder. Instead, the remainder is determined as the dividend less the product of the divisor and quotient. This fits nicely with the MLS instruction, so that the remainder of integer division is usually calculated by the following instruction sequence:

```
LDR    R0,dividend
LDR    R1,divisor
UDIV   R2,R0,R1      // R2 = quotient
MLS    R0,R1,R2,R0
// R0 = dividend - divisor x quotient
STR    R0,remainder
```

The above code is for unsigned remainders. The only change needed for signed remainders is to replace the UDIV instruction with an SDIV. The resulting code always produces a remainder that has the same sign as the dividend:

Table 5-4 Remainders produce by SDIV/MLS

Operation	Quotient	Remainder
(+14) ÷ (+3)	+4	+2
(+14) ÷ (-3)	-4	+2
(-14) ÷ (+3)	-4	-2
(-14) ÷ (-3)	+4	-2

This behavior is consistent with the C standard, which says that "If both operands are nonnegative then the remainder is nonnegative; if not, the sign of the remainder is implementation-defined."

5.5 SATURATING ARITHMETIC

When the result of an arithmetic operation exceeds the range of representation, saturating arithmetic instructions replace the result by the appropriate maximum or minimum possible value. Such instructions are used in feedback control systems, graphics, and digital signal processing of audio and video. For example, to increase the brightness of an image, you might add a constant to the three 8-bit RGB components of all the pixels in the image. Saturating arithmetic would limit the results to 255 (the maximum unsigned 8-bit value) rather than letting it wrap around to a small value and cause those pixels to appear dark. The same issue applies to audio: to increase the volume of an audio clip, you would add a constant to all of the (for example) 16-bit samples in the recording and limit the results. Saturating arithmetic can be crucial in a feedback control system where an arithmetic overflow would otherwise cause the system to fail.

Table 5-5 is a subset of the ARM Cortex-M4 instructions for saturating arithmetic. The SSAT instruction limits copies a 2's complement (signed) value from one register to another, but limits the value to the range, $-2^{n-}1$ to $2^{n-1}-1$, where n is a constant specified in the operand field of the instruction. The USAT instruction does the same for unsigned values, limiting the range to 0 to 2^n-1. The remainder of the instructions in the table limit results to the limits imposed by 8, 16 or 32-bit representations.

The saturating instructions for 8 and 16-bit signed and unsigned addition and subtraction are designed to operate on multiple values simultaneously. For example, the QADD8 instruction treats the contents of its registers as a set of four 8-bit values. It adds corresponding bytes from registers R_n and R_m and limits each 8-bit result before storing the four resulting bytes into register R_d. The instruction works this way so that you can (for example) adjust the brightness of pixels four RGB components at a time. The QADD16 instruction operates on a pair of 16-bit values in the same manner.

Table 5-5 The ARM Cortex-M4 Saturating Integer Arithmetic Instructions.

Instruction	Format		Operation	Operands
Signed Saturate	SSAT	R_d,n,Op2	$R_d \leftarrow \max(\min(-2^{n-1}, Op2), 2^{n-1}-1)$ $Op2 = R_m$ or Rm,ASR # or Rm,LSL #	1×32
Saturating Add	QADD	R_d,R_n,R_m	$R_d \leftarrow \max(\min(-2^{31}, R_n+R_m), 2^{31}-1)$	1×32
	QADD8	R_d,R_n,R_m	$R_d \leftarrow \max(\min(-2^7, R_n+R_m), 2^7-1)$	4×8
	QADD16	R_d,R_n,R_m	$R_d \leftarrow \max(\min(-2^{15}, R_n+R_m), 2^{15}-1)$	2×16
Saturating Subtract	QSUB	R_d,R_n,R_m	$R_d \leftarrow \max(\min(-2^{31}, R_n-R_m), 2^{31}-1)$	1×32
	QSUB8	R_d,R_n,R_m	$R_d \leftarrow \max(\min(-2^7, R_n-R_m), 2^7-1)$	4×8
	QSUB16	R_d,R_n,R_m	$R_d \leftarrow \max(\min(-2^{15}, R_n-R_m), 2^{15}-1)$	2×16
Unsigned Saturate	USAT	R_d,n,Op2	$R_d \leftarrow \max(\min(0, Op2), 2^n-1)$ $Op2 = R_m$ or Rm,ASR # or Rm,LSL #	1×32
Unsigned Saturating Add	UQADD	R_d,R_n,R_m	$R_d \leftarrow \max(\min(0, R_n+R_m), 2^{32}-1)$	1×32
	UQADD8	R_d,R_n,R_m	$R_d \leftarrow \max(\min(0, R_n+R_m), 2^8-1)$	4×8
	UQADD16	R_d,R_n,R_m	$R_d \leftarrow \max(\min(0, R_n+R_m), 2^{16}-1)$	2×16
Unsigned Saturating Subtract	UQSUB	R_d,R_n,R_m	$R_d \leftarrow \max(\min(0, R_n-R_m), 2^{32}-1)$	1×32
	UQSUB8	R_d,R_n,R_m	$R_d \leftarrow \max(\min(0, R_n-R_m), 2^8-1)$	4×8
	UQSUB16	R_d,R_n,R_m	$R_d \leftarrow \max(\min(0, R_n-R_m), 2^{16}-1)$	2×16

When the result of an arithmetic operation exceeds the range, saturating instructions do not set the overflow bit (the V flag), but instead set the DSP overflow and saturation flag (the Q flag) in the APSR. The Q flag may only be examined by the MRS instruction and may only be reset by the MSR instruction (see Table 5-6).

Table 5-6 ARM Cortex-M instructions for accessing the Q flag.

Instruction	Format	Operation
Move the contents of a general-purpose register into the APSR flags.	MSR APSR_nzcvq,R_n	NZCVQ ← R_n (bits 31-27) *(Bits 26-0 of PSR are unaffected)*
Move the contents of the APSR into a general-purpose register.	MRS R_d,APSR	NZCVQ → R_d (bits 31-27) *(Bits 26-0 of R_d are filled with 0's)*

PROBLEMS

1. Translate each of the following assignment statements into ARM Cortex-M4 assembly:

   (a)   int64_t   a, b ;
         a = a + b ;

   (b)   int64_t   a ;
         a -= 5 ;

   (c)   int32_t   a, b, c ;
         c = a * b ;

   (d)   uint32_t   a, b, c ;
         c = a * b ;

   (e)   int32_t   a, b, c ;
         c = a / b ;

   (f)   uint32_t   a, b, c ;
         c = a / b ;

(g)   `int32_t  a, b, c ;`

      `c = a % b ;`

PROGRAMMING PROBLEMS

2. Write a function in ARM Cortex-M4 assembly to compute the discriminant, $b^2 - 4ac$. Write a C program to test your function. The function prototype is:

```
int32_t Discriminant(int32_t a, int32_t b,
int32_t c) ;
```

3. Write a function in ARM Cortex-M4 assembly to compute the volume of a box with dimensions height, width and len. Write a C program to test your function. The function prototype is:

```
uint32_t Volume(uint32_t height, uint32_t
width, uint32_t len) ;
```

4. Write a function in ARM Cortex-M4 assembly to compute the modules function. Write a C program to test your function. The function prototype is:

```
uint32_t Modulus(int32_t number, uint32_t
   divisor) ;
```

Hint: The modulus is NOT the same as the remainder when number is negative! One approach to solve this is the following (where "%" computes the remainder):

```
modulus = ((number % divisor) + divisor) %
   divisor ;
```

CHAPTER 6

MAKING DECISIONS AND WRITING LOOPS

In ARM assembly, most decisions require a two instruction sequence. The first instruction typically performs a compare, followed by a second that branches or not based on the result of the compare. The compare is simply a subtraction that records the characteristics of its result in the flags and discards the actual value of the difference. The branch instruction then makes the actual decision to branch or not based on the value left in the flags by the compare.

6.1 COMPARE AND TEST INSTRUCTIONS

The Compare (CMP) instruction compares a register to a second operand referred to as *Op2*. The second operand may be a constant, a register, or a shifted register. There is also a Compare Negative (CMN) instruction that adds instead of subtracting the second operand.

The Test (TST) and Test Equivalence (TEQ) instructions operate in a manner similar to that of the CMP and CMN instructions. TST is like an ANDS instruction that discards the 32-bit result computed by the bitwise AND. It's usually used to determine if a single bit of a register is 1 without modifying a register. However, it can also be used to determine if any several bits of a register are all 1. The Test Equivalence (TEQ) instruction is like an EORS instruction that discards the 32-bit result computed by the bitwise Exclusive OR operation.

None of these four instructions (CMP, CMN, TST and TEQ) modify their operands. They simply update the flags, but do not require that the letter "S" be appended to the instruction mnemonic.

Table 6-1 The ARM Cortex-M4 compare and test instructions

Instruction	Syntax	Operation	Notes
Compare	CMP R_n,Op2	R_n – Op2	Update flags N,Z,C and V
Compare Negative	CMN R_n, Op2	R_n + Op2	
Test	TST R_n, Op2	R_n & Op2	Updates flags N and Z; if
Test Equivalence	TEQ R_n, Op2	R_n ^ Op2	shifted, Op2 may affect C flag

When followed by a conditional branch instruction, we interpret the CMP instruction as comparing its operands in a *left-to-right* manner. For example, consider the following instruction that compares the value in register R0 to the constant 5 and sets the flags according to the characteristics of the difference of R0 minus 5:

```
CMP     R0,5
```

This might then be followed by a conditional branch instruction that examines the flags to determine, *"is the value in R0 less than 5?"* If the answer is no, then the instruction does not branch and continues to execute instructions sequentially. If the answer is yes, however, the instruction causes execution to continue at an instruction whose address is specified by a label in the operand field of the branch.

6.2 CONDITIONAL BRANCH INSTRUCTIONS

Before the advent of structured programming[16], high-level language programmers used "goto" statements and

---

[16] "Structured programming" is a programming paradigm aimed at improving the clarity, quality, and development time of a computer program by making extensive use of subroutines, block structures, for and while

statement labels to create loops and to implement complex decisions. Today it's rare to find either a goto or a
label in a program written in a high-level language. In
assembly, however, we have no other choice – the only
way to implement loops and decisions is to use these
constructs. That's because a conditional branch instruction is exactly like an if-then statement in which the then
part is a "goto".

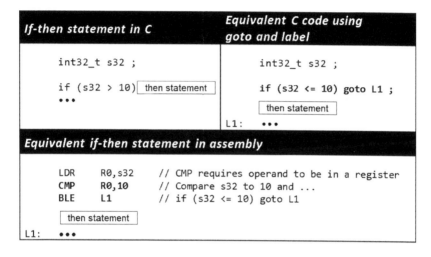

Figure 6-1 Implementing simple decisions in assembly

The BLE instruction that appears in Figure 6-1 is an example of a conditional branch instruction. Conditional
branch instructions are written as the letter "B" (for
branch) followed by a two-letter condition code. The ten
most frequently used condition codes (listed in Table 6-2)
are those used for relative magnitude comparison. Note
that except for strict equality and inequality comparisons, there are two sets of codes – one for signed operands and one for unsigned. If you're uncertain why two

---

loops—in contrast to using simple tests and jumps such as the goto statement, which could lead to "spaghetti code" that is both difficult to follow
and to maintain. (Paraphrased from Wikipedia)

separate sets are necessary, ask yourself which 4-bit integer is greater, 1101_2 or 0111_2. It depends! If interpreted as unsigned integers, they are 13_{10} and 7_{10} (respectively) and thus $1101_2 > 0111_2$; however, if interpreted as 2's complement integers, they are -3_{10} and $+7_{10}$ so that $1101_2 < 0111_2$.

Table 6-2 The ten most frequently used condition codes

Condition	Signed	Unsigned
>	GT *(Greater Than)*	HI *(Higher Than)*
>=	GE *(Greater Than or Equal)*	HS *(Higher Than or Same)*
<	LT *(Less Than)*	LO *(Lower Than)*
<=	LE *(Less Than or Equal)*	LS *(Lower Than or Same)*
==	EQ *(Equal)*	EQ *(Equal)*
!=	NE *(Not Equal)*	NE *(Not Equal)*

When coding a magnitude comparison, it's important to remember that the condition we use in assembly is usually the opposite of the condition we would have used in C. But more importantly, remember that the opposite of "less than" is "greater than or equal", *not* "greater than". In general, if a comparison includes the equality case, then the opposite comparison does not, and vice-versa!

C Source Code	Incorrect Assembly	Correct Assembly

`int32_t  s32 ;`
 	
`if (s32 > 10)`
then statement
	`    LDR R0,s32`
	`    CMP R0,10`
	`    BGT L1  // NO!`
	then statement
	
	`L1:  ...`
		`    LDR R0,s32`
		`    CMP R0,10`
		`    BLE L1  // YES!`
		then statement
		
		`L1:  ...`

Figure 6-2 Correctly choosing the opposite condition code.

Table 6-3 Complete list of ARM Cortex-M4 condition codes

Code	Meaning	Requires
EQ	Equal	Z = 1
NE	Not equal	Z = 0
CS or HS	Carry set, or unsigned ≥ ("Higher or Same")	C = 1
CC or LO	Carry clear, or unsigned < ("Lower")	C = 0
MI	Minus/negative	N = 1
PL	Plus - positive or zero (non-negative)	N = 0
VS	Overflow	V = 1
VC	No overflow	V = 0
HI	Unsigned > ("Higher")	C = 1 && Z = 0
LS	Unsigned ≤ ("Lower or Same")	C = 0 || Z = 1
GE	Signed ≥ ("Greater than or Equal")	N = V
LT	Signed < ("Less Than")	N ≠ V
GT	Signed > ("Greater Than")	Z = 0 && N = V
LE	Signed ≤ ("Less than or Equal")	Z = 1 || N ≠ V
AL	Always (unconditional)	(Rarely used)

The complete list of condition codes, and the values they require in the flags, is listed in Table 6-3. The last entry in the table is included for completeness; rather than writing the unconditional branch mnemonic as Branch Always (BAL), most people write it as simply Branch (B), without any condition code.

6.3 IF-THEN-ELSE SEQUENCES

The assembly language implementation of an if-then-else statement should always include an unconditional branch in-

struction. In Figure 6-3, the unconditional branch immediately
follows the then statement in order to skip over the else statement so that only one of the two is executed. If you omit the
unconditional branch, the processor will execute the else
statement after every execution of the then statement.

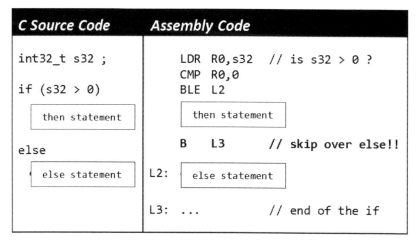

Figure 6-3 An if-then-else statement in C and assembly

When several if-then-else statements are chained together to
select and execute a single statement as shown in Figure 6-4,
every then statement should be followed by an unconditional
branch that skips over the rest of the chain.

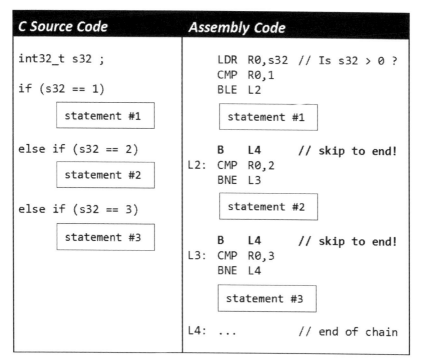

Figure 6-4 A multiple selection sequence in assembly

6.4 COMPARING 64-BIT INTEGERS

Suppose you need to compare two 64-bit unsigned integers:

```
if (u1 > u2)   then statement   else   else statement
```

One approach is to first compare the most-significant halves of the operands. If they are equal, then compare the least-significant halves:

```
        LDRD  R0,R1,u1    ; get u1 (R0 = LS Half; R1 = MS Half)
        LDRD  R2,R3,u2    ; get u2 (R2 = LS Half; R3 = MS Half)
        CMP   R1,R3       ; compare most-significant halves
        BHI   L1
        BLO   L2
        CMP   R0,R2       ; MS halves equal, so compare LS halves
        BLS   L2

L1:     [ then statement ]   ; u1 > u2

        B     L3

L2:     [ else statement ]   ; u1 <= u2

L3:            . . .
```

This can be modified to work for 64-bit signed integers s1 and s2 by changing only the first two conditional branch instructions to BGT and BLT, as in:

```
        LDRD  R0,R1,s1    ; get s1 (R0 = LS Half; R1 = MS Half)
        LDRD  R2,R3,s2    ; get s2 (R2 = LS Half; R3 = MS Half)
        CMP   R1,R3       ; compare most-significant halves
        BGT   L1
        BLT   L2
        CMP   R0,R2       ; MS halves equal, so compare LS halves
        BLS   L2

L1:     [ then statement ]   ; s1 > s2

        B     L3

L2:     [ else statement ]   ; s1 <= s2

L3:            . . .
```

However, remember that a compare is simply a subtraction that discards the difference, but records the characteristics of that result in the flags. So a more efficient approach is to simply perform a 64-bit subtraction and check the resulting flags. Not only is the code shown below faster, but it also works for unsigned simply by changing the BLE to a BLS.

```
LDRD   R0,R1,s1    ; get s1 (R0 = LS Half; R1 = MS Half)
LDRD   R2,R3,s2    ; get s2 (R2 = LS Half; R3 = MS Half)
SUBS   R0,R0,R2    ; subtract LS halves, capture the borrow
SBCS   R1,R1,R3    ; subtract MS halves w/borrow; set flags
BLE    L1
```

| then statement | ; s1 > s2

```
B      L2
```

L1: | else statement | ; s1 <= s2

L2:   . . .

6.5 IT BLOCKS

Branch instructions require the processor to flush and refill the instruction pipeline, causing performance to suffer. When a conditional branch controls a short sequence of instructions, it would be faster if there was a way you could eliminate the branch. ARM processors have the ability to fetch an instruction but make its execute phase conditional. The If-Then (IT) condition instruction provides this capability. The IT instruction individually enables or disables the execute phases of up to four instructions (called the IT block) that follow it based on a single condition.

The operand field of an IT instruction must be one of the condition codes listed in Table 6-3. Think of the letters in IT as standing for the words "If-Then", with the 'T' corresponding to the instruction immediately after the IT instruction. That instruction is enabled if and only if the condition is true. As many as three additional instructions may also be controlled by appending one to three letters to the IT mnemonic. The letter 'T' ("Then") enables the corresponding instruction if and only if the condition is true; the letter 'E' ("Else") enables an instruction if and only if the condition is false. Although it seems redundant, all instructions in the IT block must also specify their enabling condition code by appending it to their mnemonic[17].

C Source Code	Corresponding Assembly Code

`int32_t a, b, c ;`
 	
`if (a > 0) b = 1 ;`
`else c = 2 ;`
	`LDR   R0,a    // Is a > 0 ?`
	`CMP   R0,0`
	`ITTEE GT      // controls 4 instructions`
	`LDRGT R0,=1   // yes: b ← 1`
	`STRGT R0,b`
	`LDRLE R0,=2   // no: c ← 2`
	`STRLE R0,c`

Figure 6-5 Implementing an if-then-else statement with an IT block.

An instruction within an IT block may modify the flags, but this has no effect on the enabling or disabling of the remaining instructions in the block.

There are three restrictions on IT blocks:

1. An IT block may not contain a CBZ, CBNZ, CPSID, CPSIE or another IT instruction[18].

2. Only the last instructions within an IT block may modify the program counter (register PC) . This includes all branch instructions.

3. A branch to an instruction within an IT block is not allowed.

---

[17] All ARM processors use a common Unified Assembly Language (UAL). Unlike Thumb-2 instructions, appending a condition code to a regular ARM instruction makes its execution conditional without the need for an IT instruction. When assembled for a regular ARM processor, the IT instruction is ignored and the seemingly redundant requirement for condition codes appended to instructions within the IT block allows the same source code to be used for regular or Thumb-2 code.

[18] CBZ and CBNZ are discussed in a later section; CPSID is used to disable interrupts and CPSIE to enable them.

```
            .syntax  unified
            .cpu     cortex-m4
            .text
            .thumb_func
            .align   2

// uint64_t uMax64(uint64_t u1, uint64_t u2)

            .globl   uMax64

uMax64:  PUSH    {R4}       // preserve R4
         SUBS    R4,R2,R0   // perform a 64-bit subtract
         SBCS    R4,R3,R1   // set flags, discard result
         ITT     HI         // if (u2 > u1) ...
         MOVHI   R1,R3      //    then return u2 instead of u1
         MOVHI   R0,R2      //    by copying u2 into R1.R0
         POP     {R4}       // restore R4
         BX      LR         // return

         .end
```

Listing 6-1 An assembly function to find the maximum of two 64-bit unsigned values

Listing 6-1 combines what we learned in this and the previous section to create an efficient assembly language function to compare two 64-bit unsigned values. The function may be modified to compare 2's complement values by replacing the condition code HI by GT.

6.6 COMPOUND CONDITIONALS

Decisions usually begin by evaluating an expression that is either true or false. The expression, called the conditional, may be a simple comparison of two values. Compound conditionals combine one or more simple comparisons using Boolean operators. However, there are no Boolean operators in assembly. Boolean operations must therefore be converted into an equivalent arrangement of simple decisions each involving only a simple comparison as shown in Figure 6-6:

Compound Conditional in C	Rewritten with goto's and labels	Assembly Language version

```if (x > 0 && x < 9)```
 	
[then statement]
 	
```else```
 	
[else statement]
	```if (x <= 0) goto L1 ;```
	```if (x >= 9) goto L1 ;```
	[then statement]
	```goto L2 ;```
	```L1:``` [else statement]
	```L2: ...```
		```LDR R0,x```
		```CMP R0,0```
		```BLE L1```
		```CMP R0,9```
		```BGE L1```
		[then statement]
		```B L2```
		```L1:``` [else statement]
		```L2: ...```

```if (x == 0 || x == 9)```
 	
[then statement]
 	
```else```
 	
[else statement]
	```if (x == 0) goto L1 ;```
	```if (x != 9) goto L2 ;```
	[then statement]
	```L1: goto L3 ;```
	```L2:``` [else statement]
	```L3:```
		```LDR R0,x```
		```CMP R0,0```
		```BEQ L1```
		```CMP R0,9```
		```BNE L2```
		[then statement]
		```L1: B L3```
		```L2:``` [else statement]
		```L3: ...```

Figure 6-6 Implementation of compound conditional in C and assembly

Many programmers have difficulty translating compound conditionals from C to assembly correctly. If you find yourself having this problem, there is a step-by-step process that may be helpful. Consider the following: Suppose you'd like to execute a statement based on the Boolean OR of two conditions involving a signed integer. In C, you might write:

```
if (x < -100 || x > +100)
```
[then statement]

Separating this into two if statements, each with a single comparison and each controlling a goto, yields:

```
if (x < -100)  goto  L1 ;
if (x > +100)  goto  L1 ;
goto   L2 ;
```

L1: | then statement |

L2:   ...

You can eliminate one of the goto's by inverting the sense of the last comparison and changing the destination of its goto:

```
if (x <   -100)  goto  L1 ;
if (x <= +100)   goto  L2 ;
```

L1: | then statement |

L2:   ...

Then, translating into assembly, the final result becomes:

```
LDR    R0,x
CMN    R0, 100     ; if (x <  -100) goto L1
BLT    L1
CMP    R0,100      ; if (x <= +100) goto L2
BLE    L2
```

L1: | then statement |

L2:   ...

Now let's consider a compound conditional using the Boolean AND:

if (x >= -100 && x <= +100) | then statement |

This needs to be separated into two if statements that each control a goto statement. First replace the conditional by its logical inverse and modify the if statement so that it skips over the assignment (instead of executing it) when the new condition is true:

```
        if (!(x >= -100 && x <= +100)) goto L1 ;
        ┌─────────────────┐
        │ then statement  │
        └─────────────────┘
L1:    ...
```

Next, use DeMorgan's law from Boolean algebra to remove the logical NOT. To do so, replace all the logical ANDs (&&) by logical ORs (||), all logical ORs by logical ANDs (there are none in this example), and all operands (the two conditionals) by their inverse. The result is:

```
        if (x < -100 || x > +100) goto L1 ;
        ┌─────────────────┐
        │ then statement  │
        └─────────────────┘
L1:    ...
```

Now that we have a Boolean OR, it's much easier to visualize how to separate the if into two statements:

```
        if (x < -100) goto L1 ;
        if (x > +100) goto L1 ;
        ┌─────────────────┐
        │ then statement  │
        └─────────────────┘
L1:    ...
```

and thus much easier to translate into assembly language:

```
        LDR   R0,x
        CMN   R0,100        ;  if (x < -100) goto L1
        BLT   L1
        CMP   R0,100        ;  if (x > +100) goto L1
        BGT   L1
       ┌─────────────────┐
       │  then statement │
       └─────────────────┘
L1:      ...
```

6.7 WRITING LOOPS

The basic components of all loops include initialization, a test for completion, an update of variables that affect that test, and the code to be repeated (the *body* of the loop). Not every loop includes all four components. For and while loop test for completion at the top of the loop and thus repeat zero or more times; do-while loops test at the bottom of the loop and thus always repeat at least once.

All loops include an instruction to branch from the bottom to the top to continue iterating the body of the loop. In C, that branch is implicit, but it becomes explicit when translated into assembly.

```
        .syntax unified
        .cpu    cortex-m4
        .text
        .thumb_func
        .align  2

// uint32_t gcd(uint32_t u1, uint32_t u2)

        .globl  gcd

gcd:    CMP     R0,R1       // continue? (u1 != u2)
        BEQ     done
        ITE     GT          // loop body and update:
        SUBGT   R0,R0,R1    //      u1 <- u1 - u2
        SUBLE   R1,R1,R0    //      u2 <- u2 - u1
        B       gcd         // branch to top of loop
done:   BX      LR          // return: R0 = gcd(u1,u2)

        .end
```

Listing 6-2 Assembly language function to compute the greatest common divisor

Comparing a value against zero is a common test found in both if statements and in the termination/continuation test of a loop. The Thumb-2 instruction set includes two instructions just for that purpose:

Table 6-4 ARM Cortex-M4 Compare and Branch Instructions.

Instruction	Syntax	Operation
Compare and Branch if Zero	CBZ R_n,label	Branch to label If R_n=0
Compare and Branch if Non-Zero	CBNZ R_n,label	Branch to label If $R_n \neq 0$

CBZ and CBNZ combine the compare and branch decision in-to a single instruction and may be used to replace the usual two instruction sequence that compares a register against zero. The only difference is that CBZ and CBNZ do not modify the flags.

```
          CMP   R0,0        may be replaced
    by:   CBZ   R0,L1
          BEQ   L1


          CMP   R0,0        may be replaced
    by:   CBNZ  R0,L1
          BNE   L1
```

The CBZ instruction is used in Listing 6-3 as a convenient way to implement both the loop termination test and to avoid multi-plying when the parameter "n" is zero:

```
        .syntax unified
        .cpu    cortex-m4
        .text
        .thumb_func
        .align  2

// uint32_t Factorial(uint32_t n)

        .globl  Factorial

Factorial:
        LDR     R1,=1     // initialize: Factorial = 1
top:    CBZ     R0,done   // check n: Done if n is 0
        MUL     R1,R1,R0  // factorial *= n
        SUB     R0,R0,1   // decrement n and update flags
        B       top       // branch to top of loop
done:   MOV     R0,R1     // leave result in R0
        BX      LR        // return

        .end
```

Listing 6-3 Assembly language function to calculate factorial.

PROBLEMS

1. Translate each of the following C statements into a corresponding sequence of ARM Cortex-M4 instructions, where *x*, *y*, and *z* are variables of type int32_t:

   ```
   (a) z = (x < y) ? 6 : x ;
   (b) x = 0;
       for (y = 0; y < 1000; y = 2*y) x += y ;
   (c) if (x > 10) if (x < 20) y = 1 ; else z = 0 ;
   ```

2. Translate each of the following C statements into a corresponding sequence of ARM Cortex-M4 instructions without using IT blocks:

(a) `uint16_t a, b ;`

    `if (a > 0 && a < 100) b = b / 2 ;`

(b) `int32_t a, b ;`

    `if (a > 100 || a < 50) a += b ;`

3. Use an IT block to convert each of the following into a sequence of ARM Cortex-M4 Instructions:

(a) `int64_t a, b, c ;`

    `if (a > b) c = b + 2 ;`

(b) `uint64_t a, b, c ;`

    `if (a == b) c = 0 ; else c = a - b ;`

(c) `uint64_t a, b, c ;`

    `a = (b < c) ? b : c ;`

4. Translate each of the following C statements into a corresponding sequence of ARM Cortex-M4 instructions, where *ch* is the label on an 8-bit memory location whose content is an ASCII character, and *x*, *y*, and *z* are labels on 32-bit variables of type int32_t:

(a) `if (x < y && y < z) z = 6; else z = x;`

(b) `if (-10 < x && x < +10) goto L1 ;`

(c) `if (x < 10 || x > 20) y = 0 ; else y = 1 ;`

(d) `if ('a' <= ch & & ch <= 'z')`
    `    ch = ch - 'a' + 'A' ;`

(e) `x = y / 5 ;`

```
(f) uint32_t u32 ;
    int32_t s32 ;

    if (u32 > 10) s32 = s32  - 1 ;
    else s32 = s32 + 1 ;

(g) int32_t s32 ;

    if (-10 < s32 && s32 < +10) s32 = 0 ;

(h) uint32_t u32, min, max ;

    if (u32 < min || u32 > max) u32 = 0 ;
```

PROGRAMMING PROBLEMS

5. Write a function in ARM Cortex-M4 assembly language to find and return the minimum value in an array. Write a C program to test your function. The function prototype is:

```
int32_t Minimum(int32_t data[], int32_t
    count) ;
```

6. Write a function in ARM Cortex-M4 assembly language that counts the number of non-zero bits that are in its argument. (Hint: Use remainder of division by 2.) Write a C program to test your function. The function prototype is:

```
unsigned CountOnes(uint32_t word) ;
```

7. Write a function in ARM Cortex-M4 assembly language to compute the sum of products of two arrays. Write a C program to test your function. The function prototype is:

```
int32_t SumProducts(int32_t a[], int32_t
    b[], int32_t count) ;
```

8. Write a function in ARM Cortex-M4 assembly language to initialize an identity matrix of size NxN such that if j = k then A[j][k] = 1, else A[j][k] = 0. The first parameter is the address of the first element in the array. Successive elements are stored in row major format. E.g., if N = 3, the elements are store in the sequence: $A_{0,0}$, $A_{0,1}$, $A_{0,2}$, $A_{1,0}$, $A_{1,1}$, $A_{1,2}$, $A_{2,0}$, $A_{2,1}$, $A_{2,2}$. Write a C program to test your function. The function prototype is:

    ```
    void Identity(int32_t *pA, int32_t N) ;
    ```

8. Write a function in ARM Cortex-M4 assembly that inserts a byte into an array of bytes, shifting the contents to make room for the new entry. (The item that was at the end of the array is discarded.) Write a C program to test your function. The function prototype is:

    ```
    void Insert(int8_t bytes[], int32_t len,
        int8_t byte, int32_t pos) ;
    ```

    Where bytes is the name of the array, len is the number of bytes in the array, byte is the new value to be inserted, and pos is the subscript of the position where it should be inserted.

CHAPTER 7

MANIPULATING BITS

The popular phrase "crunching numbers" is often used to describe computing, and refers to performing a very large number of numerical calculations. To people who haven't programmed in assembly, this usually means arithmetic with decimal numbers. They may have never had to consider how the operations and data are implemented inside the computer and thus never dealt with the low-level details of binary representation.

However, there are lots of reasons why we need to manipulate the bits. For example, bitwise AND can be used as an efficient way to compute a remainder, to determine if an integer is an odd number, or to determine if it's divisible by (or is) a power of 2. Shifting a number left or right can be a more efficient way to multiply and divide. Calculating the address of a subscripted array reference uses a left shift to multiply the subscript by 2, 4 or 8. In fact, shifting is so common that many ARM instructions (including almost all of the arithmetic instructions) incorporate the ability to shift an operand rather than requiring a separate shift instruction.

7.1 BASIC SHIFT OPERATIONS

The contents of a register may be shifted multiple bit positions in any of five different ways, differing only in the direction of the shift and what is inserted into the "vacated" bit positions of the result.

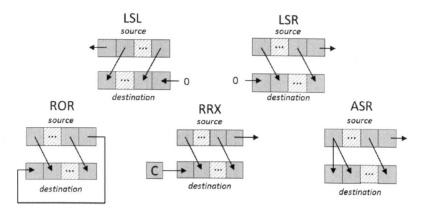

Figure 7-1 The 5 basic shift operations of the ARM processor

Logical Shift Left (LSL) is the most common type of shift. Bits are shifted left one or more positions, with 0's used to fill vacated bits on the far right. LSL is often used within the square brackets of an address specification to multiply an array subscript by 2, 4 or 8.

Logical Shift Right (LSR) is the reverse of LSL. Bits are shifted right by one or more positions, with 0's used to fill vacated bits on the far left. LSR is often used to divide an unsigned or positive value by a power of 2.

Rotate Right (ROR) shifts bits to the right by one or more positions, filling vacated bit positions on the far left with bits coming out of the far right. Although there is no rotate *left* by N bits, the same effect may be achieved by a rotate right by 32–N bits.

Rotate Right with Extend (RRX) shifts exactly one bit position to the right, filling the far-left bit position with a bit copied from the carry flag.

Arithmetic Shift Right (ASR) shifts one or more positions to the right, but leaves the far left bit unchanged. ASR is used with signed 2's complement operands. It preserves the sign of the operand as it shifts it to the right, and so can be used as a means to divide both positive and (even) negative values by a power of 2. Note that shifting right 31 times fills the result with all 0's if the operand was positive and all 1's if it was negative.

The result produced by a 1-bit ASR shift isn't exactly the same as integer division by 2. The difference occurs when the operand is a negative odd number and is due to the way in which the two operations truncate the result. Dividing ±15 by 2 should produce quotients of ±7.5, but of course integer division discards the fractional part of the result leaving only the integer part (±7). This means that division always truncates towards 0. In contrast, an arithmetic shift right truncates towards negative infinity. This difference only shows up when the operand is an odd negative number:

Table 7-1 Quotients computed by division version arithmetic right shift

Operand	Example	Correct Result	Integer Result	Binary Operand	ASR Result (Binary)	ASR Result (Decimal)
Positive & even	+10 ÷ 2	+5.0	+5	00001010	00000101	+5
Positive & odd	+11 ÷ 2	+5.5	+5	00001011	00001101	+5
Negative & even	−10 ÷ 2	−5.0	−5	11110110	11111011	−5
Negative & odd	−11 ÷ 2	−5.5	−5	11110101	**11111010**	−6

Shifts are used in three different ways by ARM Cortex-M4 instructions: (1) When specifying the address of a subscripted array element, an Logical Shift Left (LSL) is used to multiply the subscript by a power of 2 corresponding to the number of bytes per element, (2) To provide a pre-shifted copy of a register as an operand in an instruction, and (3) as a regular shift instruction. The last option is important because it is the only way that the repetition count of the shift can be provided as a variable.

Table 7-2 Three applications of shifting in the ARM Cortex-M4 instruction set

Usage	Example	Source	Amount
To multiply the subscript by the bytes per element in an subscripted array reference	LDR R2,[R0,**R1,LSL 2**]	R1	2 bits
To provide a pre-shifted copy of a register as the operand of an instruction	ADD R2,R0,**R1,ASR 31**	R1	31 bits
As a regular shift instruction	**ROR** R2,**R1,R0**	R1	specified by R0

7.1.1 Pre-Shifting Operands

The operand field of most ARM data processing instructions lists a destination register followed by two source operands. The last operand (referred to as "Op2") may be a constant, a register, or a shifted copy of a register. The register is not modified and the number of shift positions must be a constant. Any of the five basic shift operations may be used; the shift operation and the number of shift positions follow the register name and are separated from it by a comma.

The following examples illustrate how a shifting can be used to easily produce various multiples of the value held in a register without a multiply instruction. All three instructions have two operands, "R1" and "R1,LSL 2". The second operand is a copy of the content of R1 that has been shifted left twice and is equivalent to four times R1.

```
ADD  R0,R1,R1,LSL 2  // R0 = R1 + (R1 << 2) = +5*R1
RSB  R0,R1,R1,LSL 2  // R0 = (R1 << 2) - R1 = +3*R1
SUB  R0,R1,R1,LSL 2  // R0 = R1 - (R1 << 2) = -3*R1
```

7.1.2 Regular Shift Instructions

Table 7-3 lists the ARM Cortex-M4 shift instructions. Except for RRX, each instruction has three operands: the first is a destination register, the second is the register that provides the value to be shifted, and the third specifies the number of bit positions to shift, which may be a constant *or* the contents of a third register. RRX has only two operands because it can only shift by 1 bit position. Although many other instructions (e.g, ADD, ORR, etc.) can incorporate a shift of their last operand, their shift amount is restricted to a constant; the regular shift *instructions* do not have such a restriction.

In all cases, the last bit shifted out may be captured in the carry flag (C) by appending the letter 'S' to the instruction mnemonic. Note that RRXS becomes a right rotate of a 33-bit operand comprised of a 32-bit register and the 1-bit carry flag.

Table 7-3 The ARM Cortex-M4 shift instructions[19]

Instruction	Syntax	Operation	Flags	Notes
Logical Shift Left	LSL{S} R_d,R_n,*bits*	$R_d \leftarrow R_n \ll bits$	N,Z,C	Zero fills
Logical Shift Right	LSR{S} R_d,R_n,*bits*	$R_d \leftarrow R_n \gg bits$	N,Z,C	Zero fills
Arithmetic Shift Right	ASR{S} R_d,R_n,*bits*	$R_d \leftarrow R_n \gg bits$	N,Z,C	Sign extends
Rotate Right	ROR{S} R_d,R_n,*bits*	$R_d \leftarrow R_n \gg bits$	N,Z,C	right rotate
Rotate Right w/Extend	RRX{S} R_d,R_n	$R_d \leftarrow R_n \gg 1$	N,Z,C	right shift, fill w/C

---

[19] "bits" may be either a constant or a register and specifies how many bit positions to shift.

7.1.3 Multiple Precision Shifts

Shifting a 64-bit double-length operand requires a sequence of instructions. For example, one way to perform a 64-bit logical shift left is to first shift the least-significant 32 bits (the lower half) left with an LSLS, capturing bit 31 in the carry flag. Then shift the most-significant 32 bits (the upper half) left using an LSL, leaving a 0 in its least-significant bit position. Finally, use an ADC with a zero as the second operand to insert the carry flag into bit 32 of the 64-bit result.

Unfortunately, this approach won't work for a double-length shift *right* because the ADC can only be used to copy the carry flag into the least-significant bit of a register. A general-purpose approach that can be made to shift in *either* direction by any number of bit positions is illustrated in Figure 7-2 for a 1-bit right shift of a double word operand. It starts by shifting the lower half right, leaving a 0 in its most-significant bit position. Then it uses a bitwise OR to replace that 0 by the least-significant bit of the upper half. Finally, it shifts the upper half right.

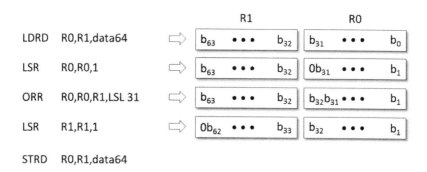

Figure 7-2 One bit logical right shift of a 64-bit operand

Sometimes there may be an even more efficient solution for a particular type of 64-bit shift. For example, the most efficient way to shift a 64-bit value left by one bit is to use addition:

```
ADDS R0,R0,R0    // Adding a value to itself is
ADC  R1,R1,R1    // the same as left shift by 1
```

Listing 7-1 provides functions to rotate a 64-bit operand left or right by one bit. These functions are simplified by limiting the shift to a single bit position. Adding a parameter to specify an arbitrary number of bit positions is more difficult, and may require a loop. Their solution is left to the reader.

```
        .syntax unified
        .cpu    cortex-m4
        .text
        .thumb_func
        .align  2

// uint64_t RotateRight64(uint64_t dword64)

        .globl  RotateRight64

RotateRight64:
        LSRS    R1,R1,1         // Shift MSW right, capture bit 32
        ORR     R1,R1,R0,LSL 31 // Insert bit 0 into bit 63
        RRX     R0,R0           // Shift LSW right, enter carry
        BX      LR              // Return

// uint64_t RotateLeft64(uint64_t dword64)

        .globl  RotateLeft64

RotateLeft64:
        ADDS    R0,R0,R0        // Shift 64-bits left by 1 bit and
        ADCS    R1,R1,R1        //    capture the MS bit in carry.
        ADC     R0,R0,0         // Insert carry into LS bit position.
        BX      LR              // Return

        .end
```

Listing 7-1 Assembly language functions to rotate a 64-bit integer 1 bit position

7.2 BITWISE INSTRUCTIONS

Bit manipulation makes extensive use of instructions that implement the machine level version of the C bitwise operators. These instructions are needed to access the data, control and status information of input/output devices, to access member elements of C structure bitfields, and to assemble and disassemble packed data that has been combined with other data in the same memory location to conserve storage. The ARM Cortex-M4 instruction set implements all of the C bitwise operations and a few more:

Table 7-4 The ARM Cortex-M4 bitwise instructions.

Instruction	Syntax		Operation	Flags
Logical AND	AND{S}	$R_d,R_n,Op2$	$R_d \leftarrow R_n$ & $Op2$	N,Z,C
Logical OR	ORR{S}	$R_d,R_n,Op2$	$R_d \leftarrow R_n$ | $Op2$	N,Z,C
Exclusive OR	EOR{S}	$R_d,R_n,Op2$	$R_d \leftarrow R_n$ ^ $Op2$	N,Z,C
Bit Clear	BIC{S}	$R_d,R_n,Op2$	$R_d \leftarrow R_n$ & ~$Op2$	N,Z,C
Logical OR NOT	ORN{S}	$R_d,R_n,Op2$	$R_d \leftarrow R_n$ | ~$Op2$	N,Z,C
Move NOT	MVN{S}	R_d,R_n	$R_d \leftarrow$ ~R_n	N,Z,C

For example, the following C statement that clears bit 5 of 'x'

```
x &= ~(1 << 5) ;
```

may be converted directly into assembly as

```
LDR  R0,x
BIC  R0,R0,0b100000 // same as BIC R0,R0,1<<5
STR  R0,x
```

Note that the binary constant 0b100000 can be written using the C expression, 1 << 5. In general, expressions using C arithmetic and bitwise operators may be used to specify a constant as long as all of their operands are constants.

One interesting application of the bitwise operators is to compute the absolute value of a signed integer without comparing to see if it's positive or negative. By eliminating the conditional branch, the processor is able to pipeline the execution of the instructions for a significant speed improvement.

The technique (see Listing 7-2) uses an Arithmetic Shift Right (ASR) to create a 32-bit sign extension of the operand. The extension has a value of -1 when the operand is negative, and 0 when the operand is positive. This value is exclusive OR'ed with, and then subtracted from the operand. When the operand is positive, the sign-extension is 0 so these two operations have no effect. But when the operand is negative, the operations produce the negative inverse of the operand.

```
        .syntax  unified
        .cpu     cortex-m4
        .text
        .thumb_func
        .align   2

// uint32_t AbsValue(int32_t s32)

        .globl   AbsValue

AbsValue:                          // s32 < 0:          else:
        EOR   R1,R0,R0,ASR 31  // R1 = ~s32        R1 = s32
        SUB   R0,R1,R0,ASR 31  // R0 = ~s32 + 1    R0 = s32
        BX    LR                   // Return

        .end
```

Listing 7-2 Assembly language function to compute absolute value

7.3 BITFIELD INSTRUCTIONS

Extraction or insertion of register bitfields whose position and width is fixed can be implemented using a single ARM Cortex-M4 instruction. There are instructions to clear a bitfield to 0's, to copy the least-significant bits of one register into a bitfield of another, or to extract an unsigned or 2's complement value from a bitfield in one register and extend it into a full 32-bit representation in another. None of the bitfield instructions listed in Table 7-5 affect the flags.

Table 7-5 The ARM Cortex-M4 bitfield instructions[20]

Instruction	Syntax	Operation	Notes
Bit Field Clear	BFC R_d,*lsb,width*	R_d<bits> $\leftarrow$ 0	
Bit Field Insert	BFI R_d,R_n,*lsb,width*	R_d<bits> $\leftarrow$ R_n<lsb's>	
Signed Bit Field Extract	SBFX R_d,R_n,*lsb,width*	R_d $\leftarrow$ R_n<bits>	Sign extends
Unsigned Bit Field Extract	UBFX R_d,R_n,*lsb,width*	R_d $\leftarrow$ R_n<bits>	Zero extends

To illustrate how these instructions are used, consider how the old Microsoft MS/DOS™ operating system packed the date and time into 32-bits, shown in Figure 7-3. To fit the date into 16 bits, it was necessary to subtract 1900 from the year and store only a 7-bit difference. And to fit the time into the lower 16 bits, the seconds were divided by two so that it could be stored using one fewer bits.

---

[20] The processor provides other bitfield instructions not listed in this table: SXTB and SXTH may be considered to be special cases of SBFX; UXTB and UXTH may be considered to be special cases of UBFX.

31	25 24	21 20	16 15	11 10	5 4	0
year - 1900	month	day	hour	minutes	secs ÷ 2

Figure 7-3 Packed representation of date and time in the MS/DOS™ operating system.

Listing 7-3 provides an assembly language implementation of a function to take the current time held in three unsigned integer parameters and return a packed 16-bit representation with separate bitfields for the hour, minutes and seconds. A similar function could be written to do the same for the date.

```
    .syntax  unified
    .cpu     cortex-m4
    .text
    .thumb_func
    .align   2


// uint16_t PackTime(uint32_t hour, uint32_t min, uint32_t sec)

    .globl   PackTime

PackTime:
    LSR    R0,R0,1      // divide the seconds by two
    BFI    R3,R0,0,5    // insert seconds/2 into bits 0-4 of R3
    BFI    R3,R1,5,6    // insert minutes into bits 5-10 of R3
    BFI    R3,R2,11,5   // insert hour into bits 11-15 of R3
    MOV    R0,R3        // Return with packed result in R0
    BX     LR


    .end
```

Listing 7-3 Assembly language function to create a packed representation of time

Listing 7-4 is a companion function also implemented in assembly that extracts the year, month and day of the month from a 16-bit packed representation of the date. The extracted values are then stored in three separate 32-bit integers at the addresses provided by the pointers provided as the last three parameters of the function. A similar function could be written to do the same for the time.

```
        .syntax  unified
        .cpu     cortex-m4
        .text
        .thumb_func
        .align   2

// void UnpackDate(uint16_t date, uint32_t *y, uint32_t *m, uint32_t *d)

        .globl   UnpackDate

UnpackDate:
    PUSH   {R4}           // Preserve the content of R4
    UBFX   R4,R0,25,7     // Extract year-1900 from bits 25-31 of R0 into R4
    ADD    R4,R4,1900     // Add 1900 to get the year
    STR    R4,[R1]        // Store the year via the pointer in 2nd parameter
    UBFX   R4,R0,21,4     // Extract the month from bits 24-21 of R0 into R4
    STR    R4,[R2]        // Store month via the pointer in 3rd parameter
    UBFX   R4,R0,16,5     // Extract the day from bits 20-16 of R0 into R4
    STR    R4,[R3]        // Store the day via the pointer in 4th parameter
    POP    {R4}           // Restore the content of R4
    BX     LR             // Return

        .end
```

Listing 7-4 Assembly language function to extract the packed date components

Unfortunately, only constants may be used for the lsb and width operands, so these instructions can't be used to create general-purpose functions with these operands as parameters. However, general purpose functions *can* be written using a sequence of other instructions and is left as an exercise for the reader.

7.4 MISCELLANEOUS BIT MANIPULATION INSTRUCTIONS

In addition to the bitwise, shift and bitfield operations, the following instructions are occasionally useful in specific situations, such as converting between little and big-endian formats when processing data held in Ethernet packets.

Table 7-6 Miscellaneous ARM Cortex-M4 bit manipulation instructions[21]

Instruction	Syntax	Operation
Count Leading Zeros	CLZ R_d,R_n	$R_d \leftarrow$ CountZeroes(R_n)
Reverse Bits	RBIT R_d,R_n	$R_d \leftarrow$ RevBits(R_n)
Reverse byte order of word	REV R_d,R_n	$R_d \leftarrow$ RevByteOrder(R_n)

7.5 BIT-BANDING

Beginning with the Cortex-M3, ARM implemented a hardware feature known as "bit-banding" that uses a portion of its 4GB address space to implement *bit*-addressable access to data in memory and peripherals.

The "***bit-band region***" is one megabyte (1 MByte) of conventional byte-addressable memory in which is each byte has a unique address.

---

[21] The processor provides several other rarely-used bit manipulation instructions not listed in this table.

The "*bit-band alias*" is a corresponding 32-megabyte (32 MByte) bit-addressable address space in which each <u>bit</u> of the bit-band region is assigned a unique *word* address (i.e., an address that is a multiple of four).

For every 8-bit byte in the bit-band region (addresses 20000000-200FFFFF$_{16}$) there are eight 32-bit words in the bit-band alias region (addresses 22000000-23FFFFFF$_{16}$).

The advantage of bit-banding is that you can access an individual bit of data using a single instruction rather than requiring a bit-manipulation sequence. For example, bit-banding allows an LDR to load a register with either 0 or 1 from a single bit in memory without AND'ing or shifting. In a similar manner, bit-banding allows an STR to write the least-significant bit of its data directly into a single bit in memory without modifying any other bits. Of course using a bit-band address with an STR requires that the *hardware* perform a read-modify-write, but only a single instruction (the STR) is fetched and executed.

Bit-banding provides an efficient way to access a set of 1-bit Boolean flags that are packed eight per byte[22]. This is particularly relevant in a multi-threaded application that may switch from one sequence of instructions to another at any moment. While a normal bit-manipulation sequence could be interrupted, bit-band access is atomic[23] because the hardware does not allow the read-modify-write operation to be interrupted, thus allowing the bits to be used as mutex objects that arbitrate access to shared data.

---

22 There is also second bit-band region (40000000-400FFFFF16) and corresponding bit-band alias (42000000-43FFFFFF16) for memory-mapped I/O devices, which facilitates access to individual bits of I/O status and control information.

23 An "atomic" operation is one that completes without interruption and thus whose computation cannot be corrupted by an interrupt routine or by another thread of computation in a multi-threaded program.

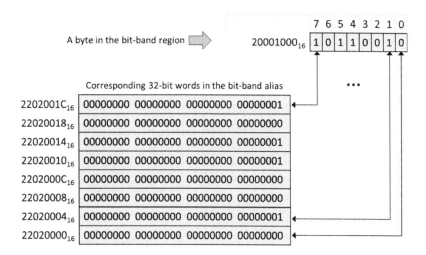

Figure 7-4 A byte in bit-band region and the corresponding bit-band alias words.

To access a particular bit in the bit-band region, calculate the corresponding bit-band alias address as:

$$\textit{bit-band alias address} = 22000000_{16} +$$
$$32 \times \textit{bit-band region offset} + 4 \times \textit{bit number}$$

where *bit-band region offset* is the address of the byte within the bit-band region that contains the bit of interest less the starting address of the bit-band region (20000000_{16}), and *bit number* is the position of the bit within the byte – i.e., a number between 0 and 7. For example, to access bit 3 of the byte at address 20001000_{16}, the bit-band alias address is calculated as:

$$\textit{bit-band alias address} = 22000000_{16} + 32_{10} \times 1000_{16} +$$
$$4 \times 3 = 2202000C_{16}$$

Address $2202000C_{16}$ allows direct access to only bit 3 of the byte at address 20001000_{16}. A read from address $2202000C_{16}$

returns a byte of all zeroes except for the least-significant bit which is a copy of the bit 3 from address 20001000_{16}. A write to address $2202000C_{16}$ ignores all but the least-significant bit of the data that is written.

Listing 7-5 is an assembly language function that uses bit-banding to change a single bit in an atomic operation. The function is given three parameters: the base address of where a collection of bits are stored within the bit-band region[24], a bit position from 0 to 8,388,607 (0 to 8 Mbits) within the bits, and the value to be written to the specified bit position.

```
        .syntax      unified
        .cpu   cortex-m4
        .text
        .thumb_func
        .align       2

// void StoreBitAtomic(void *base, uint32_t bit, uint32_t value)

// Note: 0 <= bit < 1 Mbit, value = {0,1}

        .globl       StoreBitAtomic

StoreBitAtomic:
        ADD    R0,R0,R1,LSR 3  // Add byte offset to base address
        UBFX   R3,R0,0,20      // R3 = data offset in bit-band region
        LSL    R3,R3,5         // R3 = 32 * offset
        BFI    R3,R1,2,3       // R3 = 32 * offset + 4 * (bit % 8)
        BFI    R0,R3,0,25      // Fix bits 0-24 of alias address
        LDR    R1,=1           // Need a 1 in R1 for BFI instruction
        BFI    R0,R1,25,1      // Fix bit 25 of alias address
        STRB   R2,[R0]         // Store the bit into bit-band region
        BX     LR              // Return

        .end
```

Listing 7-5 An assembly routine to implement atomic access to a single bit.

---

[24] The address may be in either the bit-band region of read/write memory or the memory-mapped bit-band region of peripheral memory.

PROGRAMMING PROBLEMS

1. Write functions in ARM Cortex-M4 assembly language that implement the following 64-bit shifts. Write a C program to test your function. The function prototypes are:

```
(a)   uint64_t LSL64(uint64_t u64) ;
(b)   uint64_t LSR64(uint64_t u64) ;
(c)   uint64_t ASR64(uint64_t u64) ;
(d)   uint64_t ROR64*uint64_t u64) ;
```

2. Write a function in ARM Cortex-M4 assembly language that returns the negative of its argument without using any subtract, negate, multiply or divide instructions. Write a C program to test your function. The function prototype is:

```
int32_t Negate(int32_t s32) ;
```

3. Write a function in ARM Cortex-M4 assembly language similar to what the Bit-Field Clear (BFC) instruction does. The function returns its first parameter, but with 0's inserted starting at a bit position given by the second parameter and a field width in bits specified by the third parameter. Write a C program to test your function. The function prototype is:

```
uint32_t BFC(uint32_t x, uint32_t lsb,
    uint32_t len) ;
```

4. Write a function in ARM Cortex-M4 assembly language similar to what the Bit-Field Insert (BFI) instruction does. The function that returns its first parameter, but with bits inserted from the second parameter starting at a bit position given by the third parameter and a

field width in bits specified by the fourth parameter. Write a C program to test your function. The function prototype is:

```
uint32_t BFI(uint32_t x, uint32_t y,
    uint32_t lsb, uint32_t len) ;
```

5. Write a function in ARM Cortex-M4 assembly language similar to what the Signed Bit Field Extract (SBFX) instruction does. The function that returns a signed 32-bit value extracted from its first parameter starting at a bit position given by the second parameter and a field width in bits specified by the third parameter. Write a C program to test your function. The function prototype is:

```
int32_t SBFX(uint32_t x, uint32_t lsb,
    uint32_t len) ;
```

6. Write a function in ARM Cortex-M4 assembly language similar to what the Unsigned Bit Field Extract (UBFX) instruction does. The function that returns an unsigned 32-bit value extracted from its first parameter starting at a bit position given by the second parameter and a field width in bits specified by the third parameter. Write a C program to test your function. The function prototype is:

```
uint32_t UBFX(uint32_t x, uint32_t lsb,
    uint32_t len) ;
```

7. Write a function in ARM Cortex-M4 assembly language that returns the number of bits within it parameter that are surrounded with leading and trailing 0's. For example, if the parameter was $006203F0_{16}$, the function

would return the value 13. Write a C program to test your function. The function prototype is:

```
uint32_t Span(uint32_t x) ;
```

8. Write a function in ARM Cortex-M4 assembly language similar to what the Reverse Byte Order (REV) instruction does, but without using that instruction. Write a C program to test your function. The function prototype is:

```
uint32_t REV(uint32_t x) ;
```

9. Write a function in ARM Cortex-M4 assembly language that given an address of a byte in the bit-band region of memory, returns the address of the word containing the bit in the bit-band alias. Write a C program to test your function. The function prototype is:

```
uint32_t *BitBandAlias(uint8_t *pByte) ;
```

CHAPTER 8

MULTIPLICATION AND DIVISION REVISITED

Some inexpensive processors don't provide multiply or divide instructions, or their execution time is longer than addition and subtraction. As Table 8-1 shows, the execution time of some ARM divides and multiplies can be a bit longer than most other instructions[25]. Fortunately, there are some very efficient ways to do multiplication and division using shift operators.

Table 8-1 ARM Cortex-M4 Instruction Clock Cycles

Instructions		Clock Cycles
PUSH, POP, LDM, STM		1 + #regs
SDIV, UDIV		2 - 12
SMLAL, UMLAL		4 - 7
SMULL, UMULL		3 - 5
Unconditional Branch (B, BL, BX)		2 - 4
Conditional Branch	Successful	2 - 4
	Failed	1
LDRD, STRD		3
ADR, MLA, MLS, & all LDR's and STR's		2
LDRB, LDRSB, LDRH, LDRSH, STR, STRB, STRH		1 - 2
All other instructions		1

---

[25] In the original Intel 8088 and 8086 processors, multiply and divide were as much as 50 times slower than add or subtract.

8.1 MULTIPLICATION USING LEFT SHIFTS

Multiplying by a power of 2 may be implemented using a simple logical shift left, and works correctly for all values of both unsigned and signed operands unless an overflow occurs:

$$A \ll k \text{ is arithmetically equivalent to } 2^k \times A$$

Multiplication by constants other than a power of 2 can be implemented using a sequence of shifts, additions, and subtractions. There is usually more than one possible sequence for any particular multiplier and the optimal choice depends on the constant's binary bit pattern. In general, patterns containing isolated 1's are best implemented using addition, while those containing a sequence of 1's are best implemented using subtraction:

Table 8-2 Optimal shift sequences for a few constant multipliers

Decimal Constant	8-bit Binary Representation	Optimal Decomposition	Number of Instructions[1]
+74	01001010	$2^6A + 2^3A + 2^1A$	3 shifts & 2 adds
+30	00111110	$2^6A - 2^1A$	2 shifts & 1 subtract
-14	11110010	$-2^4A + 2^1A$	2 shifts & 1 subtract
-17	11101111	$-2^4A - 2^0A$	1 shift & 2 subtracts

[1] A single shift instruction can typically shift an operand multiple bit positions.

Although the ARM processor has a relatively fast multiply instruction, the following example of using a shift and add sequence to multiply by 74 illustrates the principle:

```
LDR  R0,multiplicand // get multiplicand in a register
LSL  R1,R0,6          // R1 = 64*multiplicand
ADD  R1,R1,R0,LSL 3   // R1 = R1 + 8*multiplicand
ADD  R1,R1,R0,LSL 1   // R1 = R1 + 2*multiplicand
STR  R1,product       // product = (64+8+2)*multiplicand
```

8.2 DIVISION BY A POWER OF TWO

A logical shift right can be used to divide by a power of 2, but only if the dividend is not negative:

A >> k is arithmetically equivalent to $A/2^k$ when A≥0.

An arithmetic shift right of a signed 2's complement integer by 1 bit is almost the same as integer division by 2, but introduces an "off by 1" error for negative odd dividends. That's because arithmetic shift right truncates towards negative infinity while integer division truncates towards 0. The error can be corrected, however, if you add 1 to a negative dividend by one before shifting:

Table 8-3 Pre-shift adjustment to compensate for the difference in rounding between a 1-bit arithmetic shift right and integer division by 2.

Operand	Original operation	Adjusted Dividend	Binary Operand	ASR Result (Binary)	ASR Result (Decimal)
Positive & even	+10 ÷ 2	+10	00001010	00000101	+5
Positive & odd	+11 ÷ 2	+11	00001011	00000101	+5
Negative & even	−10 ÷ 2	−10	11110110	11111011	−5
Negative & odd	−11 ÷ 2	−10	11110110	11110110	−5

In general, dividing by 2^k requires that we add 2^k-1 to negative dividends before the shift. Performance will suffer, however, if this pre-shift adjustment is implemented using a conditional branch to test for a negative dividend. Processors optimize the execution of instructions that are fetched sequentially from memory because the vast majority of code is "straight-line" that does not branch. Every branch disrupts the sequential flow and slows down execution. Fortunately, there is a simple straight-line solution:

We can use a 31-bit arithmetic shift right to fill all the bits of a register with copies of the sign bit of the dividend. The result will be all 0's for positive dividends and all 1's for negative dividends. If we then AND this with the value of 2^k-1 and add it to the dividend, it will correctly compensate negative dividends and have no effect on positive dividends. For example, the way to do this in ARM assembly would be:

```
LDR  R0,dividend      // R0 = dividend
LDR  R1,k             // R1 = k (dividing by 2^k)
LDR  R2,=1            // R2 = 1
LSL  R2,R2,R1         // R2 = 2^k
SUB  R2,R2,1          // R2 = 2^k-1
AND  R2,R2,R0,ASR 31 // R2 = dividend<0 ? 2^k-1 : 0
ADD  R0,R0,R2         // pre-adjust the dividend
ASR  R0,R0,R1         // R0 = dividend / 2^k
STR  R0,quotient      // save the result
```

Although the instruction sequence above is rather long, it can be shortened to five instructions when the value of k is a constant.

8.3 DIVISION BY AN ARBITRARY CONSTANT

When the divisor is an arbitrary constant K, it's possible to use reciprocal multiplication to do the division. In principal, reciprocal multiplication simply multiplies by 1/K instead of dividing by K:

$$A \div K \qquad = \qquad A \times (1/K)$$

The problem of course is that the integer quotient of 1/K is zero for K > 1. To solve this, we multiply by the integer closest to $2^N/K$ instead of $1/K$ and then shift the result right N bits to effectively divide it by 2^N:

$$A \times (1/K) \quad = \quad [A \times (2^N/K)] \div 2^N$$
$$= \quad [A \times (2^N/K)] >> N$$

For example, suppose an unsigned variable called "dividend" contains 16 bits and we need to divide it by the constant $K=100_{10}$. The corresponding multiplier would be $2^{16}/100 = 655$ (rounded). The resulting sequence of ARM instructions would be:

```
LDRH R0,dividend // get the 16-bit dividend
LDR  R1,=655     // multiply it by 655
MUL  R2,R0,R1    // R2 contains 32-bit product
LSR  R2,R2,16    // get the most-sig. 16-bits
STRH R2,quotient // and store it as the quotient
```

Sometimes the shift can be eliminated completely by a judicious choice of N. If N is the number of bits in the operands, the double length product will contain 2N bits. Shifting the product right by N bits is equivalent to simply selecting the most-significant half of the product. For example, suppose we have a 32-bit 2's complement dividend that we want to divide by 100. The corresponding constant multiplier is $2^{32}/100 = 42,949,678$ (rounded) and the code simplifies to:

```
LDR   R0,dividend   // get the 32-bit dividend
LDR   R1,=42949678  // multiply it by 42949678
SMULL R2,R3,R0,R1   // R3.R2 contains product
STR   R3,quotient   // upper half is quotient
```

Consider how this works when the dividend contains the value $10,000_{10}$:

$$42949678 \times 10000 \;=\; 429{,}496{,}780{,}000_{10}$$
$$\text{(64-bit double-length product)}$$
$$=\; 0000\ 0064\ 0000\ C4E0_{16}$$
$$\text{(most-significant half is } 64_{16})$$
$$0000\ 0064_{16} \qquad = 100_{10}$$

Reciprocal multiplication can introduce a small error in the quotient. When $2^N/K$ is not a whole number, discarding (truncating) the fractional part provides an inexact multiplier that can introduce an error in the product and thus in the quotient. Truncating a positive multiplier will make the product smaller, but truncating a negative multiplier will actually make the magnitude of the product larger.

The magnitude of the error will be greater for large values of K. As K becomes large, the whole part of $2^N/K$ becomes smaller, which makes the loss of the fractional part that much more significant. A good guideline, therefore, is to only use reciprocal multiplication for relatively small values of K.

The error can sometimes be minimized by rounding the constant multiplier up or down. In fact the error can be eliminated completely by computing the remainder and comparing it to the divisor. The remainder can be computed fairly easily as the dividend A minus the product of K times the quotient. For unsigned or positive operands, simply add 1 to the quotient if the remainder is greater than the divisor. However, if one or more of the operands can be negative, the logic of how to correct the result is more complex. An extensive discussion of possible errors and how to minimize them appears in Hacker's Delight[26].

---

[26] Warren, Henry S., Jr., *Hacker's Delight*, 2nd ed., Addison Wesley, Pearson Education, 2013.

8.4 REMAINDER WHEN DIVIDING BY 2^K

Computing the remainder when the dividend is positive and the divisor is a power of 2 can be achieved by using a bitwise AND instead of a divide. Table 8-5 illustrates that when the divisor is a constant 2^k, AND'ing with the constant 2^k-1 produces the same result as computing the remainder. The binary pattern of 2^k-1 is a string of consecutive 1's in the least-significant bit positions; AND'ing a number with such a pattern limits the result to a number between 0 and 2^k-1.

However, the bitwise AND actually computes the modulus, not the remainder, and the two are different when the dividend is negative. The remainder X % N has the same sign as the dividend (X), but the value of X mod N is always a positive number in the range 0 to N-1. Although the results are quite different for negative dividends, in most applications the remainder is calculated from a positive dividend so that the bitwise-AND produces an equivalent result when N is a power of 2.

Table 8-4 Comparison of remainder and modulus

Remainder		Modulus (divisor = 2^k)	
+11 % 8	-11 % 8	+11 & (8 – 1)	-11 & (8 – 1)
+3	-3	+3	+5

Table 8-5 Computing remainder using a bitwise-AND

N_{10}	$N \% 8$	N_2	$(N \& 7)_2$	$(N \& 7)_{10}$
0	0	0000	0000	0
1	1	0001	0001	1
2	2	0010	0010	2
3	3	0011	0011	3
4	4	0100	0100	4
5	5	0101	0101	5
6	6	0110	0110	6
7	7	0111	0111	7
8	0	1000	0000	0
9	1	1001	0001	1
10	2	1010	0010	2
11	3	1011	0011	3
12	4	1100	0100	4
13	5	1101	0101	5
14	6	1110	0110	6
15	7	1111	0111	7

Finally, note that although the Cortex-M4F processor does have a divide instruction, computing the remainder still requires two instructions and a third to load the constant divisor, compared to a single AND instruction required for the modulus. Moreover, the divide instruction requires 2-12 processor clock cycles, while the AND only requires one.

Remainder (divisor = 8)

```
LDR R0,dividend  // get dividend
LDR R1,=8        // get divisor
DIV R2,R0,R1     // R2 = quotient
MLS R3,R1,R2,R0  // R3 = R0-R1*R2
STR R3,remainder // store result
```

Modulus (divisor=2^k,where k=3)

```
LDR R0,dividend // get dividend
AND R0,R0,0x7   // R0 = modulus
STR R0,modulus  // store result
```

Figure 8-1   Comparison of ARM code to compute remainder versus modulus

8.5 CALCULATING TRUE MODULUS WITH ARBITRARY DIVISOR

Suppose you need an alternative to the C remainder operator (%) that produces a true modulus for an *arbitrary* divisor – i.e., one that may be a variable whose value is not a power of two. A modulus is always non-negative and in the range from 0 to |divisor – 1|. You can compute the modulus from a remainder - you simply need to add the divisor to the remainder when it's negative and add nothing when it's not. Note that the sign extension of the remainder is all 1's when the remainder is negative, and all 0's when it is positive. Therefore, a quick way to compute the modulus is to AND the divisor with the sign extension of the remainder and then add the result to the remainder. An assembly language implementation of the modulus function is given in Listing 8-1.

```
        .syntax unified
        .cpu    cortex-m4
        .text
        .thumb_func
        .align  2

// uint32_t Modulus(int32_t dividend, int32_t divisor) ;

        .global  Modulus

Modulus:
        SDIV   R2,R0,R1          // R2 = quotient
        MLS    R3,R1,R2,R0       // R3 = remainder (may be < 0)
        AND    R2,R1,R3,ASR 31   // R2 = (remainder < 0) ? divisor : 0
        ADD    R0,R3,R2          // R0 = modulus (adjusted remainder)
        BX     LR                // Return

        .end
```

Listing 8-1 An assembly language function to compute the modulus

PROBLEMS

1. You can multiply register R0 by the binary constant
    01011110 using 5 shifts and 4 additions. However, you
    can reduce the total number of operations if you also
    use subtractions. Give a minimal length sequence of
    ARM Cortex-M4 instructions to do this. *(Note: This
    can be done in 3 instructions.)*

2. Give a minimal length sequence of ARM Cortex-M4
    instructions to multiply the contents of register R0 by
    each of the following values without using a multiplica-
    tion instruction.
    (a) 3
    (b) 5
    (c) 7
    (d) 9
    (e) 11

    (f) 13

3. Suppose you need to divide an unsigned 8-bit integer variable X by 9, but there is no divide instruction. If you use reciprocal multiplication, what constant should you multiply times X?

4. What integer quotient does reciprocal multiplication produce when trying to divide the 8-bit integer X by 3 when X has the value 75?

5. Suppose you need to divide an unsigned N-bit integer X by a constant K, but there is no unsigned integer divide instruction. If you use reciprocal multiplication...
    (a) Give an expression for the value of the constant multiplier.
    (b) How many bits will be in the product?
    (c) Which bits of the product hold the integer quotient?

6. Suppose you have an 8-bit processor with 8-bit registers and a single multiply instruction that produces an unsigned 16-bit product of two 8-bit operands. There is no divide instruction, so you use reciprocal multiplication when you need to divide an integer variable by a constant.
    (a) If the constant divisor is 5, what integer multiplier do you use?
    (b) If the variable contains the value 50, what will be the integer quotient?

PROGRAMMING PROBLEMS

7. Without using a divide instruction, write an ARM Cortex-M4 function to compute the <u>remainder</u> of dividing its first parameter (which may be positive or negative)

by 2^k, where k is specified by the second parameter. Write a C program to test your function. The function prototype is:

```
int32_t Remainder(int32_t s32, uint32_t k) ;
```

8. Without using a divide instruction, write an ARM Cortex-M4 function to compute the <u>modulus</u> of its first parameter (which may be positive or negative) with respect to 2^k, where k is specified by the second parameter. Write a C program to test your function. The function prototype is:

```
uint32_t Modulus(int32_t s32, uint32_t k) ;
```

CHAPTER 9

GETTING STARTED WITH FLOATING POINT

The objective of this chapter is to provide a brief introduction to the scalar operations of the floating-point unit (FPU) of the Cortex-M4 processor. We will learn on how to write C-callable functions in assembly that perform computations using real numbers. We will learn which data types and operations are supported, about the floating-point registers and which of them must be preserved by function calls, how to pass floating-point parameters and return a floating-point result, and many (but not all) of the floating-point instructions. However, there is much more to learn about floating-point computation than what is presented here.

9.1 DATA TYPES FOR REAL NUMBERS

The Cortex-M4 processor implements a subset of the full IEEE 754-2008 floating-point standard. In particular, the FPU can only perform arithmetic using *single-precision* real numbers – identical to the C data type *float*. The FPU does not support computation using double-precision reals (the C data type *double*).

Single-precision reals are stored as 32-bit values that contain a sign bit, an 8-bit exponent and a 23-bit significand. Single-precision reals can represent numbers with about six decimal digits of precision and a range of about $10^{\pm 38}$.

31 30	23 22	0
±	Exponent	Significand

Figure 9-1 Representation of the single-precision floating-point data type (float).

It's important to understand that a whole number is represented very differently in floating-point than it is as either an unsigned or 2's complement integer. For example, the bit pattern representation of the integer 1000_{10} is $000003E8_{16}$, but the bit pattern of the corresponding single-precision floating-point representation of the same value is $447A0000_{16}$. That means that any integers must be converted to floating-point to use them as operands of floating-point instructions since the FPU can only perform arithmetic on real numbers. Fortunately, the FPU does provide instructions for converting single-precision reals to and from 32-bit unsigned and two's complement integers.

9.2 FLOATING-POINT REGISTERS

The FPU contains a set of 32 registers named S0 through S31, each capable of holding a 32-bit value. When not used to hold floating-point values, they can be used as an extension of the core registers (R0 - R15) for additional temporary storage. Registers S0 through S31 may also be accessed in 64-bit pairs - as 16 registers named D0 through D15, each capable of holding a 64-bit value. Note that although the FPU has instructions for copying 64-bit values to and from the floating-point registers, it can't perform any arithmetic operations on 64-bit numbers of any type.

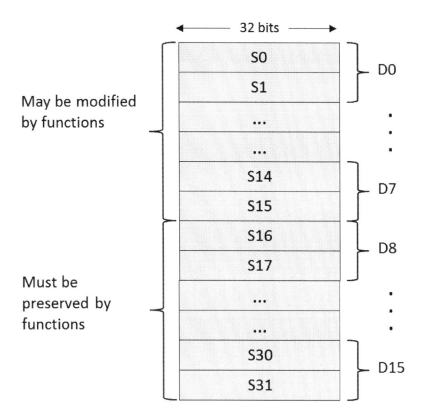

Figure 9-2 The Cortex-M4 FPU registers

The AAPCS allows S0 through S15 to be used as scratch registers that may be modified without needing to preserve their original content. However, just as the AAPCS requires functions to preserve the content of registers R4 through R11, functions must also preserve S16 through S31. The core processor's PUSH and POP instructions only work with core registers, so functions must use the FPU's VPUSH and VPOP instructions described in Table 9-1 to preserve any of the registers S16 through S31 that are modified.

Table 9-1 Instructions to PUSH and POP the FPU registers

Instruction	Syntax	Operation
Push FPU Registers	VPUSH *register list*	SP ← SP − 4 × #registers, copy registers to mem[SP]
POP FPU Registers	VPOP *register list*	Copy mem[SP] to registers SP ← SP + 4 × #registers

9.3 FUNCTION PARAMETERS AND RETURN VALUES

As many as 16 floating-point parameters may be passed to a function using FPU registers S0 through S15 in a left-to-right order starting with register S0. These floating-point parameters are in addition to any non-floating-point parameters that are passed using core registers R0 through R3; using only registers, you could theoretically pass as many as 20 parameters to a function.

Function call in C	Function call in assembly
``float Hypotenuse(float, float) ;
float side1, side2, side3 ;
•
•
•
side3 = Hypotenuse(side1, side2) ;
•
•
•```	``` •
•
•
VLDR S0,side1   // left-most param
VLDR S1,side2   // second param
BL   Hypotenuse
ADR   R0,side3   // get &save3
VSTR S0,[R0]   // save result
•
•
•```

Figure 9-3 Calling a function with floating-point parameters and return value.

Figure 9-3 is an example of how the compiler would call a function that has two float parameters and returns a result of type float. Note that register S0 is used to return a single-precision floating-point result, and that the Floating-point Store

(VSTR) instruction used to store the return value must use a core register to provide the destination address.

9.4 COPYING DATA

Listed in the tables and described in the following sections are a large variety of instructions provided by the FPU for copying data between the FPU registers, between them and the core registers, or between the FPU registers and memory. The sections that follow provide a number of examples to illustrate explain how these instructions are used.

Note that in many cases, two or more instructions use the same mnemonic, and instead use the format of their operands to specify the difference in what they do. For example, there are five different variations of the basic Move Floating Point (VMOV) instruction listed in the tables. The list is not comprehensive, however; there are a few rarely used instructions not listed in these tables.

Note that simply copying data does not change the representation of a value. For example, if you copy a two's complement integer from a core register into one of the FPU registers, it's still in a regular 2's complement integer. To convert between different representations requires that you use a FPU instruction for that purpose, discussed later in this chapter.

9.4.1 Copying a Constant into a Register

A floating-point constant is written the same way you would write a floating-point constant in C. The following are all examples of valid floating-point constants:

3.14   -1E7   +2.76E-5

Loading a floating-point constant into one of the FPU registers is supposed to be possible by using an immediate constant with a VMOV instruction, but apparently isn't supported by the assembler that comes with EmBitz:

```
VMOV  S0,3.14159          // Not currently supported!
```

Some assemblers provide a VLDR *pseudo-instruction* to load a floating-point constant, similar to the LDR pseudo-instruction, but this too is apparently unsupported by the assembler.

```
VLDR  S0,=3.14159
```

To load a floating-point constant into one of the FPU registers, use the assembler directive ".float" to create a memory location to hold the constant and then load it from memory using a real Load Floating-Point Register (VLDR) instruction:

```
pi:  .float  3.14159   // create constant in memory
       •
       •
       •
     VLDR    S0,pi     // load constant from memory
```

9.4.2 Copying One Register to Another

To copy a single 32-bit word from one FPU register to another, from a core register to an FPU register, or from an FPU register to a core register, use the Move Floating Point (VMOV) instruction:

```
VMOV  S0,S1  // Copy 32 bits from S1 to S0
VMOV  S0,R0  // Copy 32 bits from R0 to S0
VMOV  R0,S0  // Copy 32 bits from S0 to R0
```

A single VMOV instruction can also be used to copy 64 bits of data by simply adding another core register and another FPU register to the operand field:

```
VMOV  R0,R1,S0,S1  // Copy 64 bits: S1.S0 to R1.R0
VMOV  S0,S1,R0,S1  // Copy 64 bits: R1.R0 to S1.S0
```

Table 9-2 FPU instructions for copying between registers

Instruction	Syntax	Operation
Move FP Register to FP Register	VMOV S_d, S_m	$S_d \leftarrow S_m$
Move FP Register to Core Register	VMOV R_d, S_m	$R_d \leftarrow S_m$
Move Core Register to FP Register	VMOV S_d, R_m	$S_d \leftarrow R_m$
Move 2 FP Registers to Core Registers	VMOV R_t, R_{t2}, S_m, S_{m1}	$R_t \leftarrow S_m$; $R_{t2} \leftarrow S_{m1}$ Note: m1 = m + 1
Move 2 Core Registers to FP Registers	VMOV S_m, S_{m1}, R_t, R_{t2}	$S_m \leftarrow R_t$; $S_{m1} \leftarrow R_{t2}$ Note: m1 = m + 1

9.4.3 Copying from Memory to a Register

We saw earlier that the VLDR instruction can be used to copy a variable (not just a constant) from memory into an FPU register. There is also a Load Multiple FPU Registers (VLDM) instruction that can copy several words from memory in a single instruction. The operand field includes a core register used to provide the memory address, followed by a list of FPU registers. The list of registers must be a contiguous set, listed in numerical order.

Table 9-3 FPU instructions for copying from memory to registers.

Instruction	Syntax	Operation
Load single-precision FPU Register from Memory	VLDR S_d,[R_n {,constant}] VLDR S_d,label	$S_d \leftarrow mem_{32}[R_n + constant]$
Load double-precision FPU Register from Memory	VLDR D_d,[R_n {,constant}] VLDR D_d,label	$D_d \leftarrow mem_{64}[R_n + constant]$
Load Multiple FPU Registers, Increment After	VLDMIA R_n!,register list	FP registers ← memory, 1st address in R_n; Updates R_n only if write-back flag (!) is appended to R_n.
Load Multiple FPU Registers, Decrement Before	VLDMDB R_n!,register list	FP registers ← memory, addresses end just before address in R_n; Must append (!) and always updates R_n

The Load Multiple FPU Registers, Increment After (VLDMIA) instruction uses the address in the core register as a starting address that increases as FPU registers are copied from memory. The write-back flag (!) may be optionally appended to the core register name to update its content with the address following the data in memory. Note that "VLDMIA SP!,register list" is equivalent to "VPOP register list".

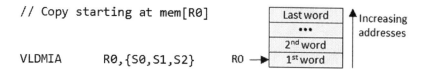

```
// Copy starting at mem[R0]

VLDMIA      R0,{S0,S1,S2}
```

The Load Multiple FPU Registers, Decrement Before (VLDMDB) instruction uses the address in the core register as that which is just beyond the memory to be copied and decreases the address as FPU registers are copied from memory.

In the case of VLDMDB, the write-back flag (!) is mandatory and the core register will always be updated.

```
// Copy ending before mem[R0]
```

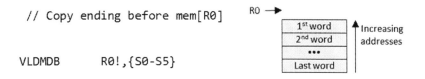

```
VLDMDB      R0!,{S0-S5}
```

9.4.4 Copying from a Register to Memory

The Store Floating-Point Register to Memory (VSTR) instruction is used to copy one of the FPU registers to memory. The address is specified as the sum of the value in a core register and an optional constant. Unfortunately, the core register is not allowed to be the program counter (PC), and this also means that the form "VSTR S_d,label" is not allowed as we saw in Figure 9-3.

There is also a Store Multiple FPU Registers (VSTM) instruction that can copy several words to memory in a single instruction. The operand field includes a core register used to provide the memory address, followed by a list of FPU registers. The list of registers must be a contiguous set, listed in numerical order.

Table 9-4 FPU instructions for copying from registers to memory

Instruction	Syntax	Operation
Store single-precision FPU Register to Memory	VSTR S_d,[R_n {,constant}	S_d → mem_{32}[R_n + constant]
Store double-precision FPU Register to Memory	VSTR D_d,[R_n {,constant}	D_d → mem_{64}[R_n + constant]
Store Multiple FPU Registers, Increment After	VSTMIA R_n!,register list	FP registers → memory, 1st address in R_n; Updates R_n only if write-back flag (!) is appended to R_n.
Store Multiple FPU Registers, Decrement Before	VSTMDB R_n!,register list	FP registers → memory, addresses end just before address in R_n; Must append (!) and always updates R_n

Similar to VLDMIA, the Store Multiple FPU Registers, Increment After (VSTMIA) instruction uses the address in the core register as a starting address that increases as FPU registers are copied to memory. The write-back flag (!) may be optionally appended to the core register name to update its content with the address following the data in memory.

```
VSTMIA R0,{S0,S1,S2} // Copy starting at mem[R0]
```

The Store Multiple FPU Registers, Decrement Before (VLDMDB) instruction uses the address in the core register as that which is just beyond the memory to be copied and decreases the address as FPU registers are copied to memory. In the case of VSTMDB, the write-back flag (!) is mandatory and the core register will always be updated. Note that "VSTMSB SP!,register list" is equivalent to "VPUSH register list".

```
VSTMDB R0!,{S0-S5}    // Copy ending before mem[R0]
```

9.5 CONVERTING BETWEEN INTEGERS AND REAL NUMBERS

We learned earlier that simply copying data between the core registers and the FPU registers does not make conversions between the corresponding floating-point and integer representations of a value. You must do that using one of the instructions listed in Table 9-5.

Converting an integer to floating-point is relatively straight-forward as long as we use the correct format for the Floating-Point Convert (VCVT) instruction according to whether the integer is unsigned or two's complement. To convert an unsigned integer to floating-point, you must append the double suffix ".F32.U32" the VCVT mnemonic, where the suffixes have a left-to-right correspondence correspond to the data type of the operands. For two's complement integers, use ".F32.S32".

Table 9-5 FPU instructions for converting between floating-point and integers

Instruction	Syntax	Operation
Convert Unsigned Integer to Floating-Point	VCVT.F32.U32 S_d,S_m	$S_d \leftarrow$ (float) S_m, where S_m is an unsigned integer
Convert 2's complement Integer to Floating-Point	VCVT.F32.S32 S_d,S_m	$S_d \leftarrow$ (float) S_m, where S_m is a 2's complement integer
Convert Floating-Point to Unsigned Integer	VCVT{R}.U32.F32 S_d,S_m	$S_d \leftarrow$ (uint32_t) S_m, rounded if optional suffix "R" is appended
Convert Floating-Point 2's to complement Integer	VCVT{R}.S32.F32 S_d,S_m	$S_d \leftarrow$ (int32_t) S_m, rounded if optional suffix "R" is appended

Converting a floating=point value to an integer representation raises the question of what to do about any fractional part in the value. If the optional "R" is omitted, the value will always be rounded towards zero, or "truncated". For example, truncating the floating-point value +3.7 produces the integer +3 and truncating the value -3.7 produces -3. If the letter "R" is appended to the VCVT mnemonic, then the floating-point value is rounded according to one of the rounding modes listed in Table 9-6.

You may be surprised to learn that there are choices when it comes to rounding. The IEEE floating-point standard defines five options, but the Cortex-M4 FPU only implements the four listed in Table 9-6. The first, "round to nearest even" (the default), is what you have probably been taught in school, but with a slight twist – the magnitude of a real number is rounded to the nearest integer, which could be either the integer just below of just above it in magnitude. However, the word "even" means that when the fractional part is exactly 0.5, then it is rounded to the nearest *even* integer.

Table 9-6 FPU rounding modes

Rounding Mode	IEEE Abbrev.	FPSCR bits 23..22	Examples -2.5	-1.5	+1.5	+2.5
Round to nearest even (default)	ToNEAR	00	-2	-2	+2	+2
Round towards positive infinity	ToPOSV	01	-2	-1	+2	+3
Round towards negative infinity	ToNEGV	10	-3	-2	+1	+2
Round towards zero (truncate)	ToZERO	11	-2	-1	+1	+2

The rounding mode is specified by bits 23 and 22 in the Floating-Point Status Control Register (FPSCR). The Move FPU System Register from ARM Core Register (VMSR) and Move ARM Core Register From FPU System Register (VMRS) instructions provide access to the rounding mode bits. We won't cover how to change the mode, however, because normally the default Round to Nearest Even and truncation are the only modes normally needed.

9.6 ARTIHMETIC WITH REAL NUMBERS

The FPU of the Cortex-M4F processor offers a rich variety of instructions for performing arithmetic on floating-point numbers. Table 9-7 is only a subset of what's available, but covers the majority of programming needs. In particular, there are a great many more variations of the multiply and add or multiply and subtract instructions than the last two instructions listed in the table.

Like the integer portion of the processor, the FPU has its own set of flags stored in the FPSCR. However, unlike the integer arithmetic instructions, most of the floating-point instructions do not affect the flags. The only exceptions are the Floating-Point Absolute Value (VABS) instruction which always clears the negative flag (N), and the Floating-Point Compare (VCMP) instruction that is described in the next section.

Table 9-7 Basic FPU arithmetic instructions

Instruction	Syntax	Operation
Floating-point add	VADD.F32 S_d,S_n,S_m	$S_d \leftarrow S_n + S_m$
Floating-point subtract	VSUB.F32 S_d,S_n,S_m	$S_d \leftarrow S_n - S_m$
Floating-point negate	VNEG.F32 S_d,S_m	$S_d \leftarrow -S_m$
Floating-point absolute value	VABS.F32 S_d,S_m	$S_d \leftarrow |S_m|$ *(clears FPU sign bit, N)*
Floating-point multiply	VMUL.F32 S_d,S_n,S_m	$S_d \leftarrow S_n \times S_m$
Floating-point divide	VDIV.F32 S_d,S_n,S_m	$S_d \leftarrow S_n \div S_m$
Floating-point square root	VSQRT.F32 S_d,S_m	$S_d \leftarrow$ square root of S_m
Fused Floating-point Multiply and Add	VFMA.F32 S_d,S_n,S_m	$S_d \leftarrow S_d + S_n \times S_m$
Fused Floating-point Multiply and Add	VFMS.F32 S_d,S_n,S_m	$S_d \leftarrow S_d - S_n \times S_m$

The simple function given in Listing 9-1 will demonstrate how to perform floating-point arithmetic. When called from a C program, the function receives two parameters of type float corresponding to the lengths of the two sides of a right triangle that are adjacent to the ninety degree angle. The function computes the length of the hypotenuse using the Pythagorean Theorem and returns the result as data of type float. Upon entering the function, the two parameters are available as the content of FPU registers S0 and S1. The return value is left in register S0.

When calling this function from a C program, it is important to include a function prototype declaration similar to the one shown in the listing. It guarantees that the parameters given to the function are of type float, forcing any necessary data type conversions before calling the function. For example, without the function prototype declaration, any parameters specified as real constants would default to type double, and any integer constants would default to type int. A similar issue applies to the return value. Without an earlier declaration (or definition) of the function, the compiler will assume that the return value is of type int.

```
      .syntax     unified
      .cpu        cortex-m4
      .text
      .thumb_func
      .align      2

// float Diagonal(float side1, float side2)

      .global     Diagonal

Diagonal:
      VMUL.F32    S0,S0,S0    // S0 = side1 * side1
      VMLA.F32    S0,S1,S1    // S0 += side2 * side2
      VSQRT.F32   S0,S0       // S0 = square root of S0
      BX          LR          // Return

      .end
```

Listing 9-1 Assembly language function to compute the diagonal of a triangle

9.7 COMPARING REAL NUMBERS

The last group of instructions we need for floating-point computing is those that compare two floating-point numbers. The Floating-Point Compare (VCMP.F32) instruction works very much like the integer CMP instruction – it forms the difference of its two operands, records the characteristics of the difference in the FPU flags, and discards the difference. Neither operand is modified – only the flags.

Table 9-8 FPU instructions needed to perform comparisons

Instruction	Syntax	Operation
Floating-Point Compare two Registers	VCMP.F32 S_d,S_m	Computes $S_d - S_m$ and updates FPU flags in FPSCR
Floating-Point Compare Register to Zero	VCMP.F32 $S_d,0$	Computes $S_d - 0$ and updates FPU flags in FPSCR
Move Flags from FPU FPSCR to core APSR	VMRS APSR_nzcv,FPSCR	Core CPU Flags ← FPU Flags

Don't forget that a floating-point compare modifies the FPU flags in the FPSCR, not those in the Application Program Status Register (APSR) of the core processor. Before you can make a branch decision based on the result of a floating-point compare, the FPU flags must be copied into the APSR using the Move Flags from FPSCR to APSR (VMRS) instruction. Important: The substring "nzcv" in the operand field of the VMRS _must_ be in lowercase!

Listing 9-2 uses a floating-point compare to implement a Maclaurin series approximation to the exponential:

$$e^x = 1 + x^1/1! + x^2/2! + x^3/3! + x^4/4! + \ldots$$

The function receives two float parameters. The first is the value of x. The second is a threshold value that determines when to stop adding terms in the series. When the next term of the series has an absolute value less than the threshold, the function returns.

```
        .syntax   unified
        .cpu      cortex-m4
        .text
        .thumb_func
        .align    2

// float eToX(float x, float minTerm)

// Parameters: S0 = x, S1 = minTerm (assume minTerm >= 0)
// Returns: Taylor series approximation of e raised to power x

// exp(x) = 1 + x + (x^2)/2! + (x^3)/3! + (x^4)/4! + ...

one:    .float    1.0

        .global   eToX

e2x:    VLDR      S2,one           // S2 = constant 1.0
        VMOV      S3,S2            // S3 = initial N = 1
        VMOV      S4,S2            // S4 = initial term = 1.0
        VMOV      S5,S2            // S5 = initial approx. = 1.0
next:   VMUL.F32  S4,S4,S0         // term = term * x
        VDIV.F32  S4,S4,S3         // term = term / N
        VABS.F32  S6,S4            // S6 = |term|
        VCMP.F32  S6,S1            // Is |term| < minDelta ?
        VMRS      APSR_nzcv,FPSCR  // Flags to APSR for testing
        BLO       done             // If yes, then done!
        VADD.F32  S5,S5,S4         // else, add the term
        VADD.F32  S3,S3,S2         // N = N + 1
        B         next             // go try the next term
done:   VMOV      S0,S5            // Copy result into S0
        BX        LR               // Return

        .end
```

Listing 9-2 Assembly language function to compute the exponential function, e^x

PROGRAMMING PROBLEMS

1. Write a function in ARM Cortex-M4 assembly language to calculate the area of a circle. Write a C program to test your function. The function prototype is:

    ```
    float  CircleArea(float radius) ;
    ```

2. Write a function in ARM Cortex-M4 assembly language to compute the dot product of two vectors. Write a C program to test your function. The function prototype is:

    ```
    float DotProduct(float vec1[], float
        vec2[], int32_t len) ;
    ```

3. Write a function in ARM Cortex-M4 assembly language to evaluate a polynomial. Write a C program to test your function. The function prototype is:

    ```
    float  Polynomial(float x, float coef[],
        int32_t terms) ;
    ```

4. Write a function in C that calls the Polynomial function developed in problem 3 to compute an eight term Taylor series approximation to the inverse, X^{-1}. (Do not use a divide!) Write a C program to test your function. The function prototype is:

    ```
    float Inverse(float x) ;
    ```

    Note: $x^{-1} = (x - 1)^0 - (x - 1)^1 + (x - 1)^2 - (x - 1)^3 + \ldots$

5. Write a function in C that calls the Polynomial function developed in problem 3 to compute an eight term Taylor series approximation to the trigonometric sine. Write a C program to test your function. The function prototype is:

```
float Sine(float radians) ;
```

Note: $sine(x) = x^1/1! - x^3/3! + x^5/5! - x^7/7! + \ldots\ldots$

6. Write a function in C that calls the Polynomial function developed in problem 3 to compute an eight term Taylor series approximation to the exponential. Write a C program to test your function. The function prototype is:

```
float Exponential(float radians) ;
```

Note: $e^x = x^0/0! + x^1/1! + x^2/2! + x^3/3! + x^4/4! + \ldots$

CHAPTER 10

WORKING WITH FIXED-POINT REAL NUMBERS

Many embedded applications don't require real numbers. When they do, fixed-point reals are often preferred over floating-point for a variety of reasons. The cost of a processor with floating-point may be too high, or using floating-point may cause an unacceptable performance penalty[27]. Although software libraries that emulate floating-point hardware are readily available, their run-time performance is typically 10 to 100 times slower than integer arithmetic or floating-point hardware. Our Cortex-M4 processor has a built-in floating-point unit for performing arithmetic with real numbers, but many other processors (particularly those found in many embedded applications) do not. When they need to perform arithmetic with real numbers, they often employ a different representation known as fixed-point reals.

10.1 Q FORMAT AND THE IMAGINARY BINARY POINT

Consider the 8-bit byte 01000111_2. It could be the ASCII code for the uppercase letter "G", the decimal integer +71, or perhaps the first byte of an instruction. How we use it determines what it represents.

Saying that it represents an integer assumes that there is an imaginary binary point at the far right of the bit pattern. The bina-

---

[27] Embedded applications are often multi-threaded and the time required to save and restore the additional registers of a floating-point unit during a context switch can significantly degrade overall system response time.

ry point is not recorded in the pattern – it's just in our head. We could just as easily think of the binary point at some other position in the pattern. For example, if we imagine the binary point in the middle of the bits, then the pattern represents the decimal value +4.4375. In effect, moving the binary point left by four bits has divided the original decimal integer value of +71 by 2^4, where the exponent corresponds to the new position of the binary point.

$$+71 \div 2^4 \; = \; +71 \div 16 \; = \; +4.4375_{10}$$

We use something called *Q format* to describe the scaling used to interpret bit patterns in this manner. The letter Q is followed by a number that indicates the number of fractional bits to the right of our imagined position of the binary point. Interpreting the pattern as an integer would correspond to a Q0 interpretation; thinking of the binary point in the middle of eight bits with four fractional bits to the right of the binary point corresponds to Q4. The following examples should make this clear:

Table 10-1 Examples of Q format.

Integer	Q	Implied	Interpretation
+71_{10}	Q0	01000111.	$+71/2^0$ = $+71.00000_{10}$
	Q3	01000.111	$+71/2^3$ = $+8.87500_{10}$
(01000111_2)	Q4	0100.0111	$+71/2^4$ = $+4.43750_{10}$
	Q5	010.00111	$+71/2^5$ = $+2.21875_{10}$

Q format optionally allows specifying the number of integer bits. The last example (Q5) in Table 10-1 would then be referred to as Q3.5 format, where the number to the left of the period indicates the number of integer bits and the number to the right of the period is the number of fractional bits. Obviously the sum of these two numbers must be the same as the total number of bits in the pattern; usually the size of the representation is understood, so the simpler Q format (e.g., Q5) is often used.

Q format works with either unsigned or 2's complement representations because it simply specifies the implied position of the binary point. Whether the integer interpretation of the value is positive or negative doesn't matter; in either case, to find the Q interpretation of the pattern, you simply divide its integer value by a power of two determined by the Q format specification:

10.2 ADDITION AND SUBTRACTION OF FIXED-POINT REALS

Fixed-point representation, with the position of the implied binary point specified using Q format, allows performing real arithmetic with the same instructions that we use for integer arithmetic. For example, adding or subtracting two fixed-point numbers using integer arithmetic simply requires that both operands use the same Q format, and produces a result with the same Q format:

Table 10-2 Fixed-point addition and subtraction of real numbers

Operand	Integer	Q	Interpretation	
A	$+30_{10}$	Q3	$+30/2^3$	$= +3.75_{10}$
B	-54_{10}	Q3	$-54/2^3$	$= -6.75_{10}$
Result	**Integer**	**Q**	**Interpretation**	
A+B	-24_{10}	Q3	$-24/2^3$	$= -3.00_{10}$
A−B	$+84_{10}$	Q3	$+84/2^3$	$= +10.50_{10}$

Two operands with different Q format must be aligned before adding or subtracting. To do this, one of the operands must be shifted. Shifting an operand left effectively multiplies it by a power of 2, and so you must be careful that the result will never overflow. Shifting an operand right arithmetically loses fractional bits off the right end that may cause a loss of precision.

We *always* have to be careful about overflow – even when the binary points are aligned. If necessary, we can avoid the overflow by shifting both operands arithmetically to the right by 1 bit position and making a corresponding note of the change in Q format. In effect, this trades one bit of precision for one more bit of range.

10.3 MULTIPLICATION AND DIVISION OF FIXED-POINT REALS

In some respects, multiplication and division are simpler because they don't require that the Q formats of their operands be the same. The total number of fractional bits in the product A×B (and thus its Q format) will simply be the sum of the number of fractional bits in each of the operands A and B.

Table 10-3 Computing the fixed-point product of 3.75×12.75

Operand	Integer	Q	Interpretation		
A	$+30_{10}$	Q3	$+30/2^3$	=	$+3.7500_{10}$
B	$+51_{10}$	Q2	$+51/2^2$	=	$+12.7500_{10}$
Result	Integer	Q	Interpretation		
A×B	$+1530_{10}$	Q5	$+1530/2^5$	=	$+47.8125_{10}$

Dividing two fixed-point real numbers is similar to reversing the multiplication process: the number of fractional bits in the quotient A÷B will be the number of fractional bits in dividend A less the number in divisor B.

Table 10-4 Computing the fixed-point quotient of 39.5 ÷ 10.375

Operand	Integer	Q	Interpretation		
A	$+1264_{10}$	Q5	$+1265/2^5$	=	$+39.5000_{10}$
B	$+83_{10}$	Q3	$+83/2^3$	=	$+10.3750_{10}$
Result	**Integer**	**Q**	**Interpretation**		
A÷B	$+15_{10}$	Q2	$+15/2^2$	=	$+3.7500_{10}$
					(Err: 1.50%)

You probably noticed that the quotient in Table 10-4 is not quite correct. The correct answer should be a bit more than 3.807_{10}. That's because integer division (1264/83) discards the fractional part of the quotient. The result can be improved by pre-shifting the original dividend to the left as much as possible before dividing, as is shown in Table 10-5. This changes the Q format of both the dividend and quotient, but provides more fractional bits in the result, and thus a more accurate result.

Table 10-5 Left-shifting the dividend to improve accuracy during fixed-point division

Operand	Integer	Q	Interpretation		
$2^3{\times}A$	$+10112_{10}$	Q8	$+10112/2^8$	=	$+39.5000_{10}$
B	$+83_{10}$	Q3	$+83/2^3$	=	$+10.3750_{10}$
Result	**Integer**	**Q**	**Interpretation**		
$(2^3{\times}A){\div}B$	$+121_{10}$	Q5	$+121/2^5$	=	$+3.78125_{10}$
					(Err: 0.682%)

A slightly better result may sometimes be obtained by adding half the divisor to the dividend before dividing as shown in Table 10-6, effectively rounding the integer quotient when its fractional part is 0.5 or more:

Table 10-6 Rounding the quotient by adding half the divisor to the dividend.

Operand	Integer	Q	Interpretation
$2^3 \times A$	$+10153_{10}$	Q8	$+10153/2^8 \ = \ +39.5000_{10}$
B	$+83_{10}$	Q3	$+83/2^3 \ = \ +10.3750_{10}$
Result	**Integer**	**Q**	**Interpretation**
$(2^3 \times A + B/2) \div B$	$+122_{10}$	Q5	$+122/2^5 \ = \ +3.81250_{10}$ *(Err: 0.138%)*

As we've just seen, the more bits that we allocate to the fractional part, the greater the precision of the representation. For any given variable, therefore, we should always choose a Q format with the largest number of fractional bits while reserving enough integer bits to provide sufficient range.

10.4 FIXED-POINT USING A UNIVERSAL Q16.16 FORMAT

Rather than having to keep track of a lot of different Q formats, wouldn't it be easier if we could use the same Q format for all fixed-point real numbers? Finding the optimum choice of Q format requires knowing what range of values our variables will have during execution. When range and resolution requirements are modest, however, a simple approach may be to use a Q16.16 format. Then fixed-point real numbers would be the same size as the fundamental word size of our 32-bit processor, making it easy to perform fixed-point arithmetic using integer operations.

Using the same Q format for all variables simplifies addition and subtraction since they no longer require pre-alignment of operands. Although multiplication doesn't require operand pre-alignment, the final single-length product must be selected from the middle bits of the double-length integer product to have the same Q format as the operands. Similarly, the original dividend must be extended with the original single-length value positioned in the middle of a double-length representation.

Recall that when you multiply two fixed-point operands together, the number of fractional digits in the product is the sum of the number of fractional digits in the two operands. For example, the double-length product of two Q16.16 numbers would therefore be in Q32.32 format.

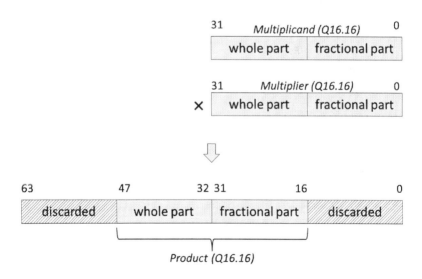

Figure 10-1 Using integer multiplication to produce a fixed-point product

To keep everything the same, we need a product in Q16.16 format. This requires selecting the middle 32 bits of the 64-bit integer product. Discarding the least-significant 16 bits simply causes some loss of precision and discarding the most-significant 16 bits imposes a maximum magnitude restriction on the operands to avoid overflow.

When you divide, the number of fractional bits in the quotient is the number in the dividend less the number in the divisor. If both the dividend and divisor have 16 fractional digits, then there would be no fractional bits in the quotient. Therefore, to produce a quotient in Q16.16 format, you have to pre-shift the dividend left by 16 bits and create a 16-bit sign extension before dividing:

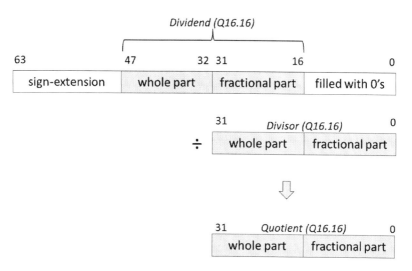

Figure 10-2 Using integer division to produce a fixed-point quotient.

Writing code to multiply or divide Q16.16 operands using a high-level language (such as C) is problematic because the arithmetic operators produce results whose data type (and thus word size) is always the same as its operands. However, writing this code in assembly is straightforward on most 32-bit processors if they have an integer multiply instruction that produces a 64-bit double-length product and an integer divide instruction that uses a 64-bit double-length dividend.

Unfortunately the range, precision or both of Q16.16 format is often insufficient. The next obvious choice is Q32.32. Addition and subtraction of Q32.32 numbers on a 32-bit processor is straight-forward, but as we will see, multiplication and division present a bit more of a challenge.

10.5 MULTIPLICATION OF Q32.32 FIXED-POINT REALS

Obviously it would be a lot easier to implement multiplication and division for the Q32.32 format using a 64-bit computer. However, 64-bit processors are far more than what is needed (and thus more expensive) for commodity embedded applications. Division is always difficult to implement efficiently – regardless of the way in which numbers are represented. However, many divisions use a constant divisor and can be replaced by multiplication using the inverse of the constant. Since multiplication is so fundamental to all arithmetic operations, we need to implement it for Q32.32 numbers using a fast algorithm written in assembler, which means using 32-bit integer operations with no loops or branching.

We know that the Q32.32 product can be taken from the middle 64 bits of a 128-bit 2's complement signed product. But don't forget that the upper half of the double-length unsigned and 2's complement products can differ. So how do you compute a 128-bit signed product on a processor who's multiply instructions at best produce 64-bit products from 32-bit operands? It turns out that it's rather easy to compute a 128-bit *unsigned* product, and also easy to convert that into a 128-bit *signed* product.

Our strategy will require doing two things: (1) devise an algorithm to compute the 128-bit product of two 64-bit *unsigned* integers and then (2) find a way to modify that result to yield the product of two *2's complement* integers. Finally, since we only need 64-bits of the 128-bit product, we will eliminate any computation that is not required for those 64 bits.

10.5.1 Computing the 128-bit Product of Two 64-bit Unsigned Integers

The value of a 64-bit unsigned integer A_U can be expressed by the following polynomial where the subscripted A's represent the individual bits of A_U:

$$A_U \quad = \quad 2^{63}A_{63} + 2^{62}A_{62} + \ldots + 2^{0}A_{0}$$

Now think of A_U as the concatenation of two 32-bit halves, and rewrite the polynomial as:

$$A_U \quad = \quad 2^{32}(2^{31}A_{63} + 2^{30}A_{62} + \ldots + 2^{0}A_{32}) + \\ (2^{31}A_{31} + 2^{30}A_{30} + \ldots + 2^{0}A_{0})$$

Let's refer to the most-significant half as A_{HI} and the least-significant half as A_{LO}:

$$\text{Let} \quad A_{HI} \quad = \quad 2^{31}A_{63} + 2^{30}A_{62} + \ldots + 2^{0}A_{32}$$
$$A_{LO} \quad = \quad 2^{31}A_{31} + 2^{30}A_{30} + \ldots + 2^{0}A_{0}$$

$$\text{Then} \quad A_U \quad = \quad 2^{32}A_{HI} + A_{LO}$$

Now express the unsigned product $A_U B_U$ in terms of A_{HI}, A_{LO}, B_{HI} and B_{LO}:

$$A_U B_U \quad = \quad (2^{32}A_{HI} + A_{LO})\,(2^{32}A_{HI} + A_{LO})$$

$$= \quad 2^{64}A_{HI}B_{HI} + 2^{32}(A_{HI}B_{LO} + A_{LO}B_{HI}) + A_{LO}B_{HI}$$

This last equation combines the results of four 64-bit partial products of 32-bit operands, each of which corresponds to a single instruction on a 32-bit processor! The only other thing we need to do is to align the partial products properly before summing. I.e., the $A_{HI}B_{HI}$ term should be shifted left by 64 bits and the middle term (in parentheses) should be shifted left by 32 bits.

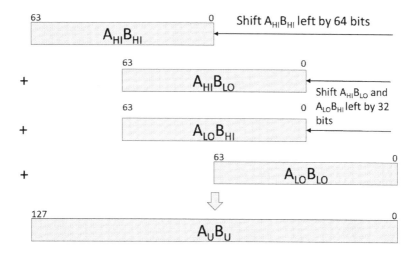

Figure 10-3 Computing the unsigned product $A_U B_U$

10.5.2 Converting an Unsigned Product into a 2's Complement Product

Recall that the unsigned and 2's complement polynomial evaluations of an N-bit binary number differ only in the sign of the most-significant bit:

$$A_U \quad = \quad 2^{N-1}A_{N-1} + 2^{N-2}A_{N-2} + ... + 2^0A_0$$
$$A_S \quad = \quad -2^{N-1}A_{N-1} + 2^{N-2}A_{N-2} + ... + 2^0A_0$$

Thus $A_S = A_U - 2^N A_{N-1}$

In other words, the 2's complement interpretation may be expressed in terms of the unsigned interpretation as follows:

$$A_S = A_U \qquad \text{when } A \geq 0$$
$$= A_U - 2^N \qquad \text{when } A < 0$$

This allows us to express the product of two 2's complement integers in terms of the corresponding unsigned interpretations:

When A,B are both ≥ 0: $A_S B_S = A_U B_U$

When only B is < 0: $A_S B_S = A_U(B_U - 2^N)$
$$= A_U B_U - 2^N A_U$$

When only A is < 0: $A_S B_S = (A_U - 2^N)B_U$
$$= A_U B_U - 2^N B_U$$

When A,B are both < 0: $A_S B_S = (A_U - 2^N)(B_U - 2^N)$
$$= A_U B_U - 2^N A_U - 2^N B_U + 2^{2N}$$

The term 2^{2N} represents a contribution which lies beyond the most significant bit of the product and may be ignored. Finally, this allows us to reach the following conclusion:

An unsigned product may be converted to a signed product by with at most two subtractions:

1.   *If A < 0, subtract all 64 bits of B from the most-significant half of the 128-bit unsigned product $A_U B_U$*

1.   *If B < 0, subtract all 64 bits of A from the most-significant half of the 128-bit unsigned product $A_U B_U$*

The conversion can be represented graphically as shown in Figure 10-4:

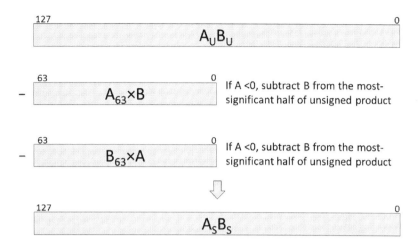

Figure 10-4 Converting an unsigned product into a signed product.

Finally, remember that we are trying to compute the product of two Q32.32 fixed point real numbers. Therefore we only need the middle 64 bits of the 128-bit signed product. In particular, when we are computing the unsigned product $A_U B_U$, we won't need the most significant 32 bits of the partial product $A_{HI}B_{HI}$ or the least-significant 32 bits of the partial product $A_{LO}B_{LO}$.

10.5.3 Example: Multiplying two Q4.4 Fixed-Point Reals

Let's illustrate signed fixed-point multiplication for Q4.4 reals using a 4-bit microprocessor whose unsigned integer multiply instruction produces an 8-bit product from two 4-bit operands.

Let $A = -1.50_{10} = 1110.1000_2$ $(A_U = 11101000_2 = 232_{10})$
Let $B = +2.75_{10} = 0010.1100_2$ $(B_U = 00101100_2 = 44_{10})$

First we must compute the 16-bit unsigned integer product $A_U B_U$, which should be $232 \times 44 = 10{,}208_{10}$

$$A_U B_U = 2^8 A_{HI} B_{HI} + 2^4 (A_{HI} B_{LO} + A_{LO} B_{HI}) + A_{LO} B_{LO}$$

$$= 2^8 (1110 \times 0010) + 2^4 (1110 \times 1100 + 1000 \times 0010) + (1000 \times 1100)$$

$$= 2^8 (00011100) + 2^4 (10101000 + 00010000) + 01100000$$

The multiplications by powers of 2 correspond to shifting left a number of bit positions specified by the exponents, thus aligning the partial products as shown below:

$A_{HI}B_{HI}$	0001	1100		
$A_{HI} B_{LO}$		1010	1000	
$A_{LO}B_{HI}$		0001	0000	
$A_{LO}B_{LO}$			0110	0000
$A_U B_U$	0010	0111	1110	0000	$= 10{,}208_{10}$

To convert this unsigned integer product to a signed 2's complement product, we need to perform at most two 32-bit subtractions. If A is negative, we subtract B from the upper half of the unsigned product. Similarly, if B is negative, we subtract A from the upper half of the unsigned product. In this example, only A is negative, so we simply subtract B:

$A_U B_U$	0010	0111	1110	0000
B	$-$ 0010	1100		
$A_S B_S$	1111	**1011**	**1110**	0000

Finally, we only need the middle 8 bits (10111110_2). Placing the binary point in the middle and converting to decimal yields:

$$1011.1110_2 = -0100.0010_2$$
$$= -4.125_{10}$$

You may have noticed that the subtractions each require a decision that implies a branch. We need to eliminate the branches to optimize performance. We'll see how to do this and eliminate any unnecessary computations in the next section.

10.5.4 An Assembly Language Implementation of Q32.32 Multiplication

Only the middle 64 bits of our 128-bit product is needed for the final result. We can use this fact to simplify the assembly language implementation of the algorithm. For example, only the most-significant half of $A_{LO}B_{LO}$ is needed, so the contents of the register that holds the least-significant half of that partial product may be discarded and the register used for another purpose. Similarly, only the least-significant half of $A_{HI}B_{HI}$ is needed, so it can be computed and added to the unsigned product using an MLA instruction.

We want our code to be as fast as possible. Our algorithm already avoids loops, but the two correction terms required to convert the unsigned product into a signed product may seem to require conditional branch instructions that would cause an instruction pipeline stall and thus delay the execution. We solve this problem for each correction by using an ASR instruction to create a 32-bit sign extension of the operand. When considered as a 32-bit integer, the sign extension will be 0 when the operand is positive and -1 when it is negative. Then an MLA instruction multiplies this value times the least-significant half of the other operand, and effectively subtracts it (or not) from the most-significant half of the result. This two-instruction ASR/MLA sequence is much faster than a conditional branch, and even faster than using an IT block. The final solution appears in Listing 10-1.

```
        .syntax      unified
        .cpu         cortex-m4
        .text
        .thumb_func
        .align       2

// int64_t Q32Product(int64_t A, int64_t B)

// A is in register pair R1.R0 (R1=MSW(A), R0=LSW(A))
// B is in register pair R3.R2 (R3=MSW(B), R2=LSW(B))

        .global      Q32Product

Q32Product:
        PUSH   {R4,R5}          // Preserve R4 and R5

        // Compute R5.R4 = middle half of 128-bit unsigned product

        UMULL  R5,R4,R0,R2   // R4.R5 = LSW(A) x LSW(B)
        LDR    R5,=0         // R5 = 0 ;
        UMLAL  R4,R5,R0,R3   // R5.R4 += LSW(A) x MSW(B)
        UMLAL  R4,R5,R1,R2   // R5.R4 += MSW(A) x LSW(B)
        MLA    R5,R1,R3,R5   // R5 += [MSW(A) x MSW(B)]<31..0>

        // Convert unsigned result to signed

        ASR    R1,R1,31      // R1 = (A < 0) ? -1 : 0
        MLA    R5,R1,R2,R5   // R5 = (A < 0) ? (R5 - LSW(B)) : R5
        ASR    R3,R3,31      // R3 = (B < 0) ? -1 : 0
        MLA    R5,R3,R0,R5   // R5 = (B < 0) ? (R5 - LSW(A)) : R5

        MOV    R0,R4         // Copy result to R1.R0
        MOV    R1,R5
        POP    {R4,R5}       // Restore R4 and R5
        BX     LR            // Return to calling program.

        .end
```

Listing 10-1 Assembly language function to multiply two
Q32.32 fixed-point real numbers.

10.6 DIVISION OF Q32.32 FIXED-POINT REALS

The division of one Q32.32 real by another can be extrapolated from the concept illustrated in Figure 10-2. To do so requires having the ability to divide a 128-bit dividend by a 64-bit divisor. What makes this difficult is that we can't build this out of the 32-bit divide instructions provided by the processor. In short, there's no great solution. About the best that one can do is to implement an iterative algorithm that computes the quotient of two 64-bit unsigned integers and encapsulate this within a wrapper function that handles the signs like the one shown in Listing 10-2.

```
extern uint64_t UQ32Quotient(uint64_t dividend, uint64_t divisor) ;

#define MSWord(x) ((int32_t *) &x)[1]

int64_t Q32Quotient(int64_t dividend, int64_t divisor)
    {
    uint64_t quotient ;
    int negate = 0 ;

    if ((MSWord(dividend) ^ MSWord(divisor)) < 0) negate = 1 ;

    if (dividend < 0) dividend = -dividend ;
    if (divisor  < 0) divisor  = -divisor  ;

    quotient = UQ32Quotient((uint64_t) dividend, (uint64_t) divisor) ;

    return negate ? -((int64_t) quotient) : (int64_t) quotient ;
    }
```

Listing 10-2 Wrapper function to compute signed integer quotient using an unsigned divide.

The function UQ32Quotient given in Listing 10-3 illustrates an algorithm for performing division with two unsigned Q32.32 fixed-point reals and served as a model for the assembly language implementation of the same algorithm given in Listing 10-4. It begins by extending the dividend to 128 bits and shifting it left by 32 bits so that the quotient will be properly aligned as a Q32.32 real. The remainder of the code simply implements a 128 by 64-bit unsigned integer division. The algorithm that it implements is by no means the fastest possible algorithm, but is perhaps one of the least complex.

```
#define MSWord(x) ((uint32_t *) &x)[1]

uint64_t UQ32Quotient(uint64_t dividend, uint64_t divisor)
    {
    uint64_t upper64, lower64 ; // 128-bit unsigned dividend
    int k, cout ;

    // Pre-scale dividend to produce Q32.32 quotient
    upper64 = (uint64_t) MSWord(dividend) ;
    lower64 = dividend << 32 ;

    for (k = 0; k < 64; k++)
        {
        // These 4 lines are a 128-bit
        // left shift with carry out
        cout = MSWord(upper64) >> 31 ; upper64 <<= 1 ;
        if (MSWord(lower64) & 0x80000000) upper64++ ;
        lower64 <<= 1 ;

        if (cout == 1 || upper64 >= divisor)
            {
            upper64 -= divisor ; lower64 += 1 ;
            if (lower64 == 0) upper64++ ;
            }
        }

    // upper64 = Remainder, lower64 = Quotient
    return lower64 ;
    }
```

Listing 10-3 C function as a model of how to do division with
Q32.32 fixed-point reals.

```
        .syntax unified
        .cpu                cortex-m4
        .text
        .thumb_func
        .align      2

// uint64_t UQ32Quotient(uint64_t dividend, uint64_t divisor)

        .global     UQ32Quotient
UQ32Quotient:
        PUSH    {R4-R6}
        LDR     R5,=0           // upper64 = MSW(dividend)
        MOV     R4,R1
        MOV     R1,R0           // lower64 = LSW(dividend) << 32
        LDR     R0,=0
        LDR     R6,=0           // k = 0
L1:  CMP     R6,64           // k < 64 ?
        BHS     L4
        LSLS    R5,R5,1         // upper64.lower64 <<= 1, C = MSbit
        ORR     R5,R5,R4,LSR 31
        LSL     R4,R4,1
        ORR     R4,R4,R1,LSR 31
        LSL     R1,R1,1
        ORR     R1,R1,R0,LSR 31
        LSL     R0,R0,1
        BCS     L2              // if C = 1, goto L2
        CMP     R5,R3           // if upper64 > divisor, goto L2
        BHI     L2
        BLO     L3
        CMP     R4,R2
        BLO     L3
L2:  SUBS    R4,R4,R2        // upper64 -= divisor
        SBC     R5,R5,R3
        ADDS    R0,R0,1         // lower64++
        ADC     R1,R1,0
        CBNZ    R0,L3           // if (lower64 == 0)
        CBNZ    R1,L3
        ADDS    R4,R4,1         //      upper64++
        ADC     R5,R5,0
L3:  ADD     R6,R6,1         // k++
        B       L1              // repeat
L4:  POP     {R4-R6}
        BX      LR              // Return (quotient in lower64)
        .end
```

Listing 10-4 Assembly language function to divide two 64-bit unsigned integers.

PROGRAMMING PROBLEMS

For each of the following problems, use a C #define or typedef to create a data type called Q32 capable of holding a fixed-point Q32.32 real.

1. Write a C function that returns a constant of type Q32, computed from the ratio of two integers without using any floating-point operations. Write a C program to test your function. The function prototype is:

   ```
   Q32 BuildQ32Constant(int32_t dividend,
       int32_t divisor) ;
   ```

2. Write a C function that prints a Q32 number as a real number without using any floating-point operations. Write a C program to test your function. The function prototype is:

   ```
   void PrintQ32(Q32) ;
   ```

3. Use the function developed in problem C H A P T E R 0 to create two Q32 values, 12.34 and -56.78 and write a C program compute and display their sum and difference.

4. Write a C function to calculate the area of a circle using Q32 fixed-point reals and the multiply and divide routines of Figure 10-1 and Figure 10-4. Write a C program to test your function. The function prototype is:

   ```
   Q32 CircleArea(Q32 radius) ;
   ```

5. Write a C function to compute the dot product of two vectors using Q32 fixed-point reals and the multiply and divide routines of Figure 10-1 and Figure 10-4. Write a C program to test your function. The function prototype is:

```
Q32 DotProduct(Q32 vec1[],Q32 vec2[],
    int32_t len) ;
```

6. Write a C function to evaluate a polynomial using Q32 fixed-point reals and the multiply and divide routines of Figure 10-1 and Figure 10-4. Write a C program to test your function. The function prototype is:

```
Q32 Polynomial(Q32 x, Q32 coef[], int32_t
    terms) ;
```

7. Write a function in C that calls the Polynomial function developed in problem 3 to compute an eight term Taylor series approximation to the inverse, X^{-1}. (Do not use a divide!) Write a C program to test your function. The function prototype is:

```
Q32 Inverse(Q32 x) ;
```

   Note: $x^{-1} = (x-1)^0 - (x-1)^1 + (x-1)^2 - (x-1)^3 + \ldots$

8. Write a function in C that calls the Polynomial function developed in problem 3 to compute an eight term Taylor series approximation to the trigonometric sine. Write a C program to test your function. The function prototype is:

```
Q32 Sine(Q32 radians) ;
```

   Note: $\text{sine}(x) = x^1/1! - x^3/3! + x^5/5! - x^7/7! + \ldots\ldots$

9. Write a function in C that calls the Polynomial function developed in problem 3 to compute an eight term Taylor series approximation to the exponential. Write a C program to test your function. The function prototype is:

```
Q32 Exponential(Q32 radians) ;
```

Note: $e^x = x^0/0! + x^1/1! + x^2/2! + x^3/3! + x^4/4! + \ldots$

CHAPTER 11
INLINE CODE

One of the goals of this text is to improve the run-time performance of a program. The approach we've used up until this point is to implement time-critical sections of code as functions written in assembly to be called from a C program. Sometimes, however, just the overhead of the function call and return (and the pipeline stalls they cause) can cancel any benefit obtained by coding in assembly. There are two ways to eliminate the call-return overhead – inline functions and inline assembly.

11.1 INLINE FUNCTIONS

The inline keyword is used with functions to cause their code to be replicated everywhere the function is called, thus eliminating the call-return overhead at the expense of a larger program size. Such functions are usually also static functions since making them inline requires that the function definition resides in the same C source code file where the function is called. For example, given the function definition:

```
static inline int Add1(int a) { return a + 1 ; }
```

then the following "function call" would produce an instruction sequence similar to the third column of Table 11-1 rather than the Branch and Link (BL) sequence shown in the second column.

Table 11-1 Comparing calls to inline and non-inline functions

Function Call	If Add1 is NOT an inline function	If Add1 IS an inline function

y = Add1(x) ;	LDR R0,x
	BL Add1
	STR R0,y
		LDR R0,x
		ADD R0,R0,1
		STR R0,y

11.2 INLINE ASSEMBLY

It's also possible to avoid the call-return overhead by embedding assembler instructions directly amongst lines of C code. This technique is known as *inline assembly* and is supported by GNU compilers such as ours.

Inline assembly is more difficult to use than simply writing a function in assembly. Since inline code is embedded within a C function, it is subject to all of the compiler optimization strategies including the way registers are allocated and used, the possible rearrangement of the order in which lines of code appear, or even the elimination of code that that compiler deems unnecessary. Of course there are workarounds for these problems, but it adds a layer of complexity that is not a concern when code is written as an assembly language function rather than inline with other lines of C code.

To insert assembler instructions into a C program, you must use either *basic asm* or *extended asm*. A basic asm statement has the following format, where the square brackets indicate that the volatile keyword (explained later) is optional:

```
asm [volatile] ( AssemblerInstructions ) ;
```

AssemblerInstructions is one or more instructions written as literal strings separated by whitespace. All but the last instruction string should end with a newline (\n) and tab (\t) character to format the instructions consistent with the output of the compiler, as in:

```
asm (  "MOV R0,R1              \n\t"
       "ADD R0,R0,1") ;
```

Although basic asm statements are easier to write, extended asm is necessary in order to interact correctly with the optimizer of the compiler to produce smaller, safer and more efficient code. Extended asm has the following format:

```
asm [volatile] (    AssemblerTemplate
    : OutputOperands
    [ : InputOperands
    [ : Clobbers ] ] ) ;
```

Note that square brackets are used to indicate optional components and colons are used to separate components inside the parentheses. *OutputOperands* may be omitted, but the first colon is required; omitting them and all of the subsequent optional components changes the asm statement to *basic asm*.

The ***AssemblerTemplate*** component is similar to the AssemblerInstructions component of basic asm except that each instruction is actually a template with options regarding how the compiler may specify each of its operands.

11.2.1 Input and Output Operands

Think of the InputOperands and OutputOperands components as a description of how the inline instructions in the AssemblerTemplate connect to data in the C program. I.e., InputOperands identifies variables, function parameters or even C expressions whose values are used as source operands by the inline instructions and OutputOperands identifies variables used as destination operands. It isn't necessary to write instructions to load an input variable into a register, nor to store the result back into a C variable. All of that is handled by the compiler and allows it to take advantage of values that may already be in registers, or to keep an intermediate result in a register because the following C code needs to use it. The inline code simply defines what's required to perform the desired computation.

The **OutputOperands** component is optional. It is a comma separated list of entries, each consisting of three parts: an identifier surrounded by square brackets preceded by a percent sign, a constraint string, and a C expression surrounded by parentheses in the following format:

%[*identifier*] "=r" (*expression*)

The identifier matches those used in the AssemblerTemplate. In the simplest form, the C expression is simply another identifier that is the name of a variable or function parameter in the C program. The two identifiers may be the same or different.

The optional **InputOperands** component has the same format as the OutputOperands component.

We'll discuss the Clobbers component later. For now, let's consider the following simple example:

```
int result, value, numbits ;
...
value = ... ;
numbits = ... ;

asm ("ASR %[operand1],%[operand2],%[operand3]"
    : [operand1] "=r" (result)// OutputOperands
    : [operand2] "r"  (value),// InputOperands
      [operand3] "r"  (numbits)
) ;

printf("%d ASR %d = %d\n", value, numbits, result) ;
```

Notice how the OutputOperands and InputOperands components establish a one-to-one correspondence between the identifiers referenced in the instruction to variables and parameters in the C code. You may find it simpler to make the inline identifiers the same as the C identifiers, writing the asm statement as:

```
asm ("ASR %[result],%[value],%[numbits]"
    : [result]  "=r" (result) // OutputOperands
    : [value]   "r"  (value), // InputOperands
      [numbits] "r"  (numbits)
) ;
```

11.2.2 Constraints and Modifiers

The constraint string defines what the instruction requires as an operand. Our ARM processor uses what's known as a *Load-Store Architecture*, which means that the only instructions that may reference memory are variants of the LDR and STR instructions. Since the compiler takes care of loading and storing the operands of inline code, the constraint strings usually specify that the operand be a register, with the letter 'r' for a core register or the letter 'w' for a floating-point register.

Register constraints may be prefixed by a constraint *modifier*. By default, a register is considered to be read-only (an input).

However, prefixing it with an equals sign (=) indicates that it is write-only (an output), while prefixing it with a plus sign (+) indicates that it is read/write – i.e., that it may be used not only as an output, but also used as an input value later in the same sequence of inline instructions.

Table 11-2 Inline assembly constraint modifiers.

Modifier	When used as a prefix to 'r' or 'f' ...
=	A register used as the destination operand of an instruction.
+	A register used both as a destination operand and (later) as a source operand.
&	An output register that should not be a reused input register – usually because later code in the asm statement still needs one or more of the input operands.

Many ARM Cortex-M4 instructions such as ADD, ORR, LSL, etc., allow their last operand to be either a core register or an integer constant. You can specify a constraint that allows an operand to be either a core register or a constant by combining them in the constraint string, as in "ir". Although there are several other constraint options, Table 11-3 lists those that are most common for the ARM Cortex-M4.

Table 11-3 Inline assembly constraints.

Constraint	Operand is allowed to be ...
r	One of the core registers (R0 through R15)
w	One of the floating-point registers (S0 through S31)
i	An integer constant
X	Any kind of operand is allowed

11.2.3 Allowing Constants or Registers as Operands

Consider the following inline "stub" function that uses inline assembly for its code:

```
static inline
int32_t ASR(int32_t value, uint32_t numbits)
{
int32_t result ;

asm ("ASR %[result],%[value],%[numbits]"
    : [result]  "=r" (result) // OutputOperands
    : [value]   "r"  (value), // InputOperands
      [numbits] "ir" (numbits)
) ;

return result ;
}
```

By adding the constraint specifier "i" to numbits, it allows the compiler to use a constant as the last operand of the ASR instruction as shown in the second column of Table 11-4; without it, that operand can only be a register, requiring the compiler to generate an additional instruction to load the constant into a second register.

Table 11-4 Advantage of allowing additional constraint options.

Function Call	Constraint = "ir"	Constraint = "r"

y = ASR(x, 5) ;	LDR R0,x
	ASR R0,R0,5
	STR R0,y
		LDR R0,x
		LDR R1,=5
		ASR R0,R0,R1
		STR R0,y

11.2.4 The Clobbers Component

The optional Clobbers component is a comma-separated list of items modified by instructions in the AssemblerTemplate, in addition to anything modified as an output. The compiler needs this information to know about any possible side effects of the asm statement. For example, the following asm statement clears the flags in the APSR. Similar to a function with no parameters or return value, this asm statement has no OutputOperands or InputOperands. However, it does modify register R0 and the flags, and thus both must be listed in the Clobbers component. Note that "cc" is used to indicate that the flags are modified, and although an uppercase 'R' can be used in a register name in the AssemblerTemplate, a lowercase 'r' is required in register names that appear in the Clobbers component.

```
asm (
    "LDR  R0,=0           \n\t"  // Clear the flags
    "MSR  APSR_nzcvq,R0"        // Copy R0 to APSR
    :                           // No OutputOperands
    :                           // No InputOperands
    : "cc", "r0"                // Clobbers R0 and
flags
) ;
```

Rather than requiring the use of register R0 to provide the new value for the flags, it would have been better to let the compiler select the best register to use. One way to do this is to declare a temporary variable in C, load it with the constant, and then reference its identifier in the asm statement. The compiler will generate the same code, but is now free to select a register other than R0 to hold the constant.

```
uint32_t temp ;

temp = 0 ;

asm (
    "MSR  APSR_nzcvq,%[temp]" // Clear the flags
    :                         // No OutputOperands
    : [temp] "r" (temp)       // InputOperands
    : "cc"                    // Clobbers only flags
) ;
```

Other than register names and the "cc" indicator for the flags, the only other item that might appear in the Clobbers list is "memory". This item is used when instructions in the Assembler Template modify memory locations other than those listed in the OutputOperands, such as a location whose address is held in a pointer that is one of the InputOperands.

11.2.5 Working with 64-bit Operands

Suppose you'd like to write some inline code to perform an arithmetic shift right on a 64-bit integer. You know how to do this in two instructions, one for each 32-bit half of the integer, but how do you reference the two halves? Recall that the last item listed in an InputOperand may be any valid C expression surrounded by parentheses. You can use that to write a cast expression that makes the compiler treat a 64-bit integer as an array of two 32-bit words. The following example performs an arithmetic shift right on the 64-bit integer called "src" and stores the result in the 64-bit integer "dst". The expression takes the address of the integer, which is normally considered to be the address of a 64-bit integer, casts that as a pointer to a 32-bit integer, and then applies subscripting to the pointer to access one of the two 32-bit halves.

```
int64_t orig, half ;

asm (
    "ASRS %[dstHi],%[srcHi],1   \n\t"
    "RRX  %[dstLo],%[srcLo]         "
  : [dstLo] "=r" (((uint32_t *) &dst)[0]),
    [dstHi] "=r" (((uint32_t *) &dst)[1])
  : [srcLo] "r"  (((uint32_t *) &src)[0]),
    [srcHi] "r"  (((uint32_t *) &src)[1])
  : "cc"
) ;
```

11.3 THE OPTIONAL VOLATILE KEYWORD

The volatile keyword is sometimes necessary in order to avoid
certain compiler optimizations that may modify, move, or even
discard your code and cause the program to behave unexpect-
edly. However, this doesn't mean you should simply always
use the volatile keyword. Doing so may prevent the compiler
from applying legitimate optimizations that improve the run-
time performance of your program. In general, if your asm
statement performs some simple calculation with no side effects, then don't use the volatile keyword. However, if your
code contains side-effects that must occur where you placed
your asm statement, and should not be moved or discarded,
then use the volatile keyword.

Suppose for example, that you use an asm statement to create
an instruction whose only purpose is to provide a time delay as
in the following example:

```
int k, temp ;

for (k = 0; k < 10000; k++)
    {
    asm (  "MOV %[temp],%[temp]"
            : [temp] "+r" (temp)
    ) ;
    }
```

The optimizer will think that the MOV instruction isn't doing
any useful work and will completely remove the asm statement
and would probably remove the for loop as well. By adding the
volatile keyword, you disable this optimization and keep the
MOV instruction and the loop.

11.3.1 Using Artificial Dependencies

There are certain situations in which the optimizer can move
other code relative to your asm statement in a manner that can
cause a problem. Suppose you use inline assembly to change
the floating-point rounding mode to truncate just before a line
of C code that performs a floating-point addition:

```
float series, term ;
uint32_t temp ;
...
asm volatile (
    "VMRS %[temp],FPSCR                 \n\t"
    "ORR  %[temp],%[temp],0x3 << 22  \n\t"
    "VMSR FPSCR,%[temp]                 "
    : [temp] "+r" (temp)

    :

    :
) ;
series += term ;
```

Even if the asm statement isn't moved, it's still possible that the
compiler might move the addition, placing it just before the
asm statement, thus causing the wrong rounding mode to be

used. This can be solved by introducing an artificial dependen-
cy in the asm statement:

```
asm volatile (
    "VMRS  %[temp],FPSCR                   \n\t"
    "ORR   %[temp],%[temp],0x3 << 22 \n\t"
    "VMSR  FPSCR,%[temp]                   "
          : [temp] "+r" (temp), "=X" (series)
          :
          :
) ;
```

PROGRAMMING PROBLEMS

1. Write an asm statement to reverse the order of the bytes
    within a 32-bit C variable named "x32".

2. Write an asm statement to right rotate the contents of a 64-
    bit C variable named "x64" by 1 bit position.

    Method 3:

3. Write an asm statement that returns a count of the number
    of leading zeroes in the 32-bit C variable named "x32".

4. Write an inline stub function in C to perform a Bit Field
    Clear with an asm statement that uses the BFC instruction.
    Require the starting bit position and field width to be speci-
    fied as integers so that the function call may be replaced by
    a single BFC instruction. The function prototype is:

```
static inline uint32_t BFC(uint32_t word,
    int lsb, int len) ;
```

5. Write an inline stub function in C to perform a Bit Field
   Insert with an asm statement that uses the BFI instruction.
   Require the starting bit position and field width to be specified as integers so that the function call may be replaced by
   a single BFI instruction. The function prototype is:

   ```
   static inline uint32_t BFI(uint32_t dst,
       uint32_t src, int lsb, int len) ;
   ```

6. Write an inline stub function in C to perform a Signed Bit
   Field Extract with an asm statement that uses the SBFX instruction. Require the starting bit position and field width
   to be specified as integers so that the function call may be
   replaced by a single SBFX instruction. The function prototype is:

   ```
   static inline int32_t SBFX(uint32_t word,
       int lsb, int len) ;
   ```

7. Write an inline stub function in C to perform an Unsigned
   Bit Field Extract with an asm statement that uses the UBFX
   instruction. Require the starting bit position and field width
   to be specified as integers so that the function call may be
   replaced by a single UBFX instruction. The function prototype is:

   ```
   static inline uint32_t UBFX(uint32_t word,
       int lsb, int len) ;
   ```

CHAPTER 12

PROGRAMMING PERIPHERAL DEVICES

Most microcontroller applications do not require a large amount of memory for storing instructions or data. However, modern processors have a 32-bit address that can directly reference any location in a four gigabyte address space. There is so much unused address space that some of it is assigned to peripheral devices. This "memory-mapped I/O" design allows programmers to use C pointers to access a device, and makes it possible to apply the regular C operators to test I/O status bits and to set or clear control bits.

Microcontroller chips combine a processor, memory and a number of peripheral devices all within a single device. To maximize flexibility, they provide a large number of configuration options to specify how the external pins of the device are connected to the internal peripheral devices, to select which internal data path is used to connect it to the processor, and to configure all the operating parameters of the device. As a result, peripheral devices typically require a significant amount of initialization code that is usually implemented in C rather than assembly.

Manufacturers of microcontrollers create extensive software libraries to access the microcontroller peripherals. These libraries implement C-callable functions that are much easier to use than trying to program a peripheral in assembly. In this chapter, however, we will look at a few simple examples at a relatively low level to get an idea of what is required to initialize

and use these devices. As always, our approach will involve a
mix of C and assembly.

The peripheral devices used as examples in this chapter are not
necessarily available in all microcontrollers based on the ARM
Cortex-M4 processor. They are available, however, in the microcontroller used in the STMicroelectronics 32F429I-DISCO
Discovery board that is the target platform described in this
book. ARM has defined a large number of optional peripheral
components and each manufacturer chooses those that will be
combined with the processor and memory on a particular microcontroller chip.

Peripheral devices usually transfer data at rates that are significantly slower than the processor's ability to process it. For example, many devices process data at rates measured in thou-
sands of bytes per second, such as the data from an analog-to-
digital converter or serial modem. By comparison, the processor is capable of accessing memory more than 100 million
times per second. Thus any software that communicates with a
peripheral device must somehow synchronize the processor
access to the slower data rate of the device.

There are four possible ways that peripheral devices may be
programmed. The various options differ with respect to maximum data transfer rate, response time (latency), the amount of
additional hardware required, and the complexity of the software. The choice may depend on multiple factors, such as how
the hardware of the peripheral's interface was designed, what
options are supported by the microcontroller, and what performance constraints are required for a particular application. In
this chapter we will consider four options and develop code
both in C and in assembly that illustrates each method.

There is an enormous amount of information needed to be able
to program peripheral devices due to the large number of dif-

ferent devices available, each with a large number of data, control and status interfaces. Rather than try to incorporate all of that detail here, the interested reader should obtain copies of the microcontroller documentation[28,29].

12.1 BLOCKING I/O: CRC32 PERIPHERAL

Blocking I/O is a hardware design in which processor instructions that transfer data to or from a peripheral will stall until the device is ready. Instead of taking the normal one or two processor clock cycles to execute, the instruction may take several clock cycles. Since the delay can be detrimental to the processor's ability to respond to other events, the blocking I/O is rarely used unless the maximum delay is never more than (say) one to five clock cycles.

The CRC32 peripheral in the STM32F429 microcontroller uses blocking I/O. Specifically, attempts to write to the data register of the device (CRC_DR) will stall until the current CRC computation has completed, thus allowing back-to-back writes or consecutive write and read accesses.

12.1.1 The Basic CRC Algorithm

The 32-bit cyclic redundancy check (CRC32) code is used to detect errors in the transmission of information. CRC32 find use in Ethernet packets, MPEG-2 video files, PNG image files, and several other applications.

---

[28] *STM32F3 and STM32F4 Series Cortex®-M4 programming Manual* (PM0214), Rev. 4, STMicroelectronics, May 2014.

[29] *STM32F405/415, STM32F407/417, STM32F427/437 and STM32F429/439 advanced ARM®-based 32-bit MCUs* (RM0090), STMicroelectronics, Rev 11, October 2015.

Listing 12-1 is a C implementation of the CRC32 algorithm adapted from a listing found in the book, *Hacker's Delight*[30]. There are much faster ways to implement the algorithm, but this is the clearest illustration of the basic algorithm and will serve as a model for implementing our own version.

```c
uint32_t crc32(void *data, uint32_t bytes)
    {
    uint8_t *pu8 = (uint8_t *) data ;
    uint32_t crc = 0xFFFFFFFF ;     // Initial value

    while (bytes-- != 0)
        {
        // Zero-extend and reverse bit order of input data
        uint32_t u32 = ReverseBits((uint32_t) *pu8++) ;

        for (int k = 0; k < 8; k++)  // Update the CRC
            {
            if (((crc ^ u32) & 0x80000000) != 0)
                {
                crc = (crc << 1) ^ 0x04C11DB7 ;
                }
            else crc = crc << 1 ;

            u32 = u32 << 1 ;
            }
        }

    return ~ReverseBits(crc) ; // Reverse & invert final result
    }
```

Listing 12-1 The basic CRC32 algorithm.

All CRC algorithms use the same basic algorithm, but differ in a number of ways. Besides differences in the polynomial they use to calculate the CRC, some algorithms initialize the CRC

---

[30] Warren, Henry S., Jr., *Hacker's Delight,* 2nd ed., Addison Wesley, Pearson Education, 2013.

value to zero and others to all ones. Some require reversing the bits in the data before and after calculating the CRC, and some invert all the bits in the final result while others don't. The "standard" CRC32 algorithm shown in Listing 12-1 and used in Ethernet packets uses the polynomial[31] designated by $04C11DB7_{16}$, sets the initial value to all ones, reverses[32] bits and inverts the result.

12.1.2 A Hardware-Assisted Implementation in C

The STM32Fxxx series of microcontrollers can calculate the CRC32 code much faster by taking advantage of their built-in CRC calculation hardware. The CRC32 unit has a single 32-bit read/write data register (CRC_DR). Every time you write data to it, it updates the CRC by combining the new data with the previous CRC value. Every time you read data from the data register, you get the latest CRC value that has been calculated.

Listing 12-2 is a C function that calculates the standard CRC32 using the CRC peripheral in the STM32Fxxx series of micro-controllers. The code illustrates how symbolic constants and cast operators may be used to create pointers to the memory-mapped registers of a peripheral device so that they may be manipulated using the regular C operators. The volatile key-word is used to inform the compiler that the device may change the contents of the data register independent of the pro-gram so that the usual optimization rules should not be applied.

The bit reversals shown in Listing 12-2 could be avoided if the CRC calculation was modified to shift left and use a polynomi-al constant in which the bits have been reversed. However, the

---

[31] The polynomial is written as the sum of powers of "x" corresponding to those bits in the constant that are equal to 1. E.g., $04C11DB7_{16}$ is the poly-nomial $x^{32}+x^{26}+x^{23}+x^{22}+x^{16}+x^{12}+x^{11}+x^{10}+x^8+x^7+x^5+x^4+x^2+x^1+x^0$.

[32] The details of how to reverse the bits of a 32-bit word are not relevant to the CRC algorithm and thus the code for function ReverseBits has been omitted.

shift and the polynomial are implemented in the hardware of the STM32F429 processor and cannot be changed, so our hardware-assisted CRC function must include the bit reversals.

The hardware automatically forces the initial value to all 1's when the unit is reset at the beginning of the calculation. The polynomial does not appear in the code because it's hard coded to the same $04C11DB7_{16}$ value inside the CRC peripheral.

```c
#define pCRC_DR    ((volatile uint32_t *)   0x40023000)
#define pCRC_CR    ((uint32_t *)            0x40023008)
#define pRCC_AHB1ENR ((uint32_t *)          0x40023830)

uint32_t crc32(void *data, uint32_t bytes)
    {
    uint32_t crc, crc_reg, *p32 = data ;

    *pRCC_AHB1ENR |= 1 << 12 ;     // Enable CRC clock
    *pCRC_CR |= 0x00000001 ;       // Reset the CRC calculator

    while (bytes >= 4)
        {
        *pCRC_DR = ReverseBits(*p32++) ;
        bytes -= 4 ;
        }

    crc_reg = *pCRC_DR ;
    crc = ReverseBits(crc_reg) ;

    if (bytes > 0)
        {
        uint32_t bits = 8 * bytes ;
        uint32_t xtra = 32 - bits ;
        uint32_t mask = (1 << bits) - 1 ;

        *pCRC_DR = crc_reg ;

        *pCRC_DR = ReverseBits((*p32 & mask) ^ crc) >> xtra ;
        crc = (crc >> bits) ^ ReverseBits(*pCRC_DR);
        }

    return ~crc ;
    }
```

Listing 12-2 Basic CRC32 algorithm using the CRC peripheral in the STM32F429

Before you can use the CRC peripheral, you must enable the clock signal that drives the CRC calculation by setting bit 12 of the microcontroller's RCC AHB1 peripheral clock register (RCC_AHB1ENR) to 1. You must then initialize the CRC calculator by setting the least-significant bit of the Control Register of the CRC peripheral (CRC_CR) to 1, which also loads the data register with an initial value of $FFFFFFFF_{16}$. The RCC, CRC_CR and CRC_DR registers are actually memory-mapped to addresses 40023830_{16}, 40023008_{16} and $0x40023000_{16}$, respectively. To access them, we cast each address constant as a pointer to a 32-bit unsigned integer and then dereference the pointers to read or write the registers. This is done using the #define statements at the beginning of Listing 12-2.

There is one major difference between the basic software algorithm of Listing 12-1 and the hardware-assisted algorithm of Listing 12-2 – the latter processes data 32 bits at a time, while the basic software algorithm processes data only one byte at a time. The if statement seen in Listing 12-2 treats the case when the number of data bytes is not a multiple of four.

12.1.3 A Hardware-Assisted Implementation in Assembly

Now that we have a high-level version of the hardware-assisted CRC function, we can now more easily rewrite it in assembly. Although the assembly version will likely be only marginally faster than the code in Listing 12-1, it is still an appropriate next step since we're trying to create the fastest possible CRC32 calculation.

Converting our C version to assembly is rather straight-forward but somewhat tedious. The two function parameters - the pointer to the data and the number of bytes of data, are received in registers R0 and R1 and kept in those registers for most of the code. However, once the while loop has processed all the full 32-bit words of data and arrives at the if statement (label L2), the remaining byte count in register R1 is used to calculate three values required to update the CRC with any partial data remaining: the number of data bits (bits), a bit mask (mask), and a shift amount (xtra).

Throughout the code, register R2 is used as a pointer to the memory-mapped registers of the CRC peripheral. At the beginning, R2 is loaded with the bitband address of bit 12 of register RCC_AHB1ENR to enable the CRC clock, and then loaded with the bitband address of bit 0 of register CRC_CR to initialize the CRC peripheral. These bits must be set without changing the other bits of the registers. By using bit banding, we save a total of four instructions compared to what would have been required to implement the bitwise-OR used in Listing 12-2.

Once the initializations are done, R2 is loaded with the address of the CRC data register (CRC_DR) and left that way for the rest of the code. Registers R3 and R4 are required as scratch registers for temporary values, which in turn required that the original content of R4 be preserved by pushing it onto the stack at entry and restored by popping it from the stack just before the return.

Fortunately, the Cortex-M4 provides an instruction (RBIT) to reverse all the bits in a 32-bit register, so our assembly language version is able to do each bit reversal with a single instruction.

```
            .cpu        cortex-m4
            .text
            .thumb_func
            .align      2

            .global     crc32

crc32:  PUSH    {R4}
        LDR     R3,=1
        LDR     R2,=0x42470630    // Use bit band address to
        STR     R3,[R2]           //    enable the CRC Clock
        LDR     R2,=0x42460100    // Use bit band address to
        STR     R3,[R2]           //    reset the CRC unit
        LDR     R2,=0x40023000    // R2 = pCRC_DR
L1:     CMP     R1,4              // while (bytes >= 4)
        BLO     L2                // {
        LDR     R3,[R0],4         //    R3 = *p32++ ;
        RBIT    R3,R3             //    R3 = ReverseBits(R3)
        STR     R3,[R2]           //    *pCRC_DR <-- R3
        SUB     R1,R1,4           //    bytes -= 4
        B       L1                // }
L2:     LDR     R3,[R2]           // crc_reg (R3) <-- *pCRC_DR
        RBIT    R4,R3             // crc (R4) = ReverseBits(R3)
        CBZ     R1,L3
        STR     R3,[R2]           // *pCRC_DR <-- crc_reg
        LSL     R3,R1,3           // bits (R3) = bytes << 3
        LDR     R1,=1             // R1 = 1
        LSL     R1,R1,R3          // R1 = 1 << bits
        SUB     R1,R1,1           // mask (R1) = R1 - 1
        LDR     R0,[R0]           // R0 = *p32
        AND     R0,R0,R1          // R0 &= mask
        EOR     R0,R0,R4          // R0 ^= crc
        RBIT    R0,R0             // R0 = ReverseBits(R0)
        RSB     R1,R3,32          // xtra (R1) = 32 - R3
        LSR     R0,R0,R1          // R0 >>= xtra
        STR     R0,[R2]           // *pCRC_DR <-- R0
        LDR     R0,[R2]           // R0 <-- *pCRC_DR
        RBIT    R0,R0             // R0 = ReverseBits(R0)
        LSR     R4,R4,R3          // R4 = crc >> bits
        EOR     R4,R0,R4          // R4 = (crc >> bits) ^ R0
L3:     MVN     R0,R4
        POP     {R4}
        BX      LR
        .end
```

Listing 12-3 Assembly function to calculate CRC32 on STM32Fxxx microcontroller.

12.2 POLLED WAITING LOOP: RANDOM NUMBER GENERATOR

Polled waiting loop is an I/O programming technique in which the processor repeatedly executes instructions that test to see if the peripheral device is ready before transferring any data. Although it creates an opportunity for the processor to perform other computations between successive polls, the ability of the processor to quickly respond to changes in the status of the device may be adversely affected if the run-time of that computation is excessive.

The random number generator in the STM32F429 microcontroller provides a status register that contains a bit that is set to 1 when a new random number becomes available. When the processor reads the number from the device, the bit is automatically reset to 0 until the next random number becomes available. This allows the processor to repeatedly test this bit to synchronize its attempts to read numbers from the device.

Random number generators are used in a variety of applications such as game software based on cards or dice, statistical sampling algorithms, simulation and generating cryptographic keys. The random number generator built into all members of the STM32 family of microcontrollers uses a continuous analog noise source to produce random 32-bit integers that meet the stringent requirements of the National Institute of Standards and Technology (NIST)[33].

The random number generator consists of three memory-mapped 32-bit registers - a control register (RNG_CR), a status register (RNG_ST), and a data register (RNG_DR). To use the device, you must first enable the random number generator's clock source and then enable the random number generator it-

---

[33] FIPS PUB 140-2, *Security Requirements for Cryptographic Modules*. National Institute of Standards and Technology, October 2001.

self. To enable the clock source, set RNGEN (bit 6) of the AHB2 peripheral clock enable register (RCC_AHB2ENR). To enable the random number generator, set RNGEN (bit 2) in the control register. When a random number is desired, you must wait until DRDY (bit 0) of the status register is 1, indicating that the next random number is available in the data register[34].

```c
#define pRCC_AHB2ENR    ((uint32_t *)            0x40023834)
#define pRNG_CR         ((uint32_t *)            0x50060800)
#define pRNG_SR         ((volatile uint32_t *) 0x50060804)
#define pRNG_DR         ((volatile uint32_t *) 0x50060808)

void RNG_Initialize(void)
    {
    *pRCC_AHB2ENR  |= (1 << 6) ;   // Enable RNG clock src
    *pRNG_CR       |= (1 << 2) ;   // Enable RNG peripheral
    }

uint32_t RNG_ReadValue(void)
    {
    while ((*pRNG_SR & 1) == 0) /* Polled waiting loop */ ;
    return *pRNG_DR ;
    }
```

Listing 12-4 C functions for using polling to access the random number generator.

Listing 12-4 shows two C functions that may be used to access the random number generator. Although the equivalent assembly code appears in Listing 12-5, it is provided only for completeness because neither efficiency nor code size is normally a concern when using this device. Although bit banding could have been used to enable the random number generator clock, it would only have saved one instruction. However, even though it requires setting a single bit, bit banding could not be used to enable the random number generator peripheral because the address of the device is not within a bit band region.

---

[34] The random number generator monitors the validity of the data using two bits in the status register that are not covered in this example.

```
        .syntax  unified
        .cpu     cortex-m4
        .text
        .thumb_func
        .align   2

// void RNG_Initialize(void) ;

        .global  RNG_Initialize

RNG_Initialize:
        LDR     R1,=0x42470698  // Address of RCC_AHB2ENR
        LDR     R0,[R1]
        ORR     R0,R0,1 << 6    // Enable RNG clock source
        STR     R0,[R1]

        LDR     R1,=0x50060800  // Address of RNG_CR
        LDR     R0,[R1]
        ORR     R0,R0,1 << 2    // Enable RNG peripheral
        STR     R0,[R1]
        BX      LR              // Return

// uint32_t RNG_ReadValue(void) ;

        .global  RNG_ReadValue
RNG_ReadValue:
        LDR     R1,=0x50060804  // Address of RNG_SR
Poll:   LDR     R0,[R1]         // Poll: Check to see if a new
        TST     R0,1            //    random number is available.
        BEQ     Poll
        LDR     R1,=0x50060808  // Address of RNG_DR
        LDR     R0,[R1]         // Read a new random number
        BX      LR              // Return

        .end
```

Listing 12-5 Assembly functions for using polling to access the random number generator.

12.3 INTERRUPT-DRIVEN: TIMER TICK

Input/output programming is all about timing. Events occur at unpredictable times, such as the arrival of an Ethernet packet, the press of a key on the keyboard, or the completion of an analog-to-digital conversion that now has data available to be read. Software should be designed to not only respond to these events, but to do so with as little delay (latency) as possible. In severe cases, too much delay can allow the arrival of new data that overwrites the previous data (data loss) before the processor was able to accept it. Rather than waiting for a lengthy computation to complete, interrupts allow the processor to suspend the current computation, respond to the interrupt by executing a function to collect the data from the interrupting device, and then return to the suspended program and continue from where it left off. The function typically reads the data from the device and stores it in a queue to be processed at a later time.

An interrupt can be requested by an input device when it has data ready for the processor to read, by an output device that has finished processing a transfer and is ready to receive new data, or simply by an event with no associated data, such as the periodic "tick" of a timer to keep track of time.

An interrupt is a special type of event called an *exception*. In addition to interrupts, exceptions include reset, fault conditions, and the execution of SVC instructions used to make operating system calls. Each exception has an associated exception number, a priority level, an exception handler, and an entry in the vector table that contains the addresses of the exception handlers. The vector table resides at a memory location defined by the contents of the processor's *Vector Table Offset Register* (VTOR).

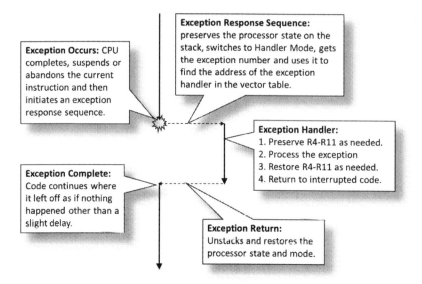

Figure 12-1 Exception Processing.

Regardless of the type of exception, the processor responds by performing the following actions:

1. **Suspends execution of the current program**. The current instruction is allowed to complete if only one clock cycle is required. Instructions that transfer multiple words to or from memory (such as LDM, STM, PUSH and POP) are suspended to be continued after the interrupt has been processed. All other instructions are abandoned and restarted after the interrupt.

2. **Preserves the processor "state" on the stack**. This is called "*stacking*", and includes the contents of the Program Status Register (the PSR, which includes the APSR), the return address, and the contents of registers R0 through R3, R12 and LR.

3. **Switches from Thread Mode to Handler Mode**. This change is recorded by setting bit 24 (the T bit) of the Program Status Register. The change in mode affects

the behavior of instructions that modify the Program Counter (PC) to trigger "unstacking" (restoring the processor state) after the exception is processed.

4. **Transfers control to the appropriate exception handler.** The processor uses the exception number to retrieve the address of the exception handler from the *Vector Table.*

Exception processing is designed so that exception handlers can be written like any other function – even written in C. The handler may safely modify the contents of the Processor Status Register (PSR) and registers R0 through R3 since the exception response preserved their original contents on the stack. If writing a handler in assembly, PUSH and POP instructions must be used as usual to preserve any other registers that it modifies.

The BX LR instruction used to return behaves differently when the processor is in Handler Mode; rather than simply copying the content of the Link Register (LR) into the Program Counter (PC), the BX LR gets its return address from the stack and performs unstacking to restore the processor state. Note that unstacking restores the previous content of the PSR, which includes the previous value of the T bit and thus the previous mode (Thread Mode or Handler Mode).

Listing 12-6 is a program that illustrates interrupt-driven programming using a simple periodic timer tick to measure time. After calling the InitializeHardware function to perform the usual setup, the main program executes a number of statements to configure the timer. In general, all peripheral devices require a clock signal to operate. To reduce power consumption, these clock signals are turned off by default after a reset. Therefore the first statement in the configuration sequence turns on the clock to the timer.

The next two statements determine the rate at which interrupts are generated. The processor clock runs at 180 MHz (180,000,000 cycles per second). It goes through a *prescaler* that we program to divide that rate by 18,000 to feed the counter that's inside the timer with a 10 KHz (10,000 cycles per second) clock. This signal increments the counter once on every cycle of the 10 KHz clock. When the counter reaches a programmed value of 999, it generates an interrupt request, resets to 0 and continues counting. This process repeats itself ten times every second. The remaining three statements configure other parameters, enabling the counter to interrupt, enabling it to count, and unmasking its interrupt signal. Finally, the asm statement is used to turn on the interrupt system of the processor. The main program then enters an infinite loop that prints the value of global variable "tenths" every time it changes.

The timer's exception handler is the function named TIM2_IRQHandler. Its main purpose is to increment the value of tenths. However, it also has to clear the interrupt request before returning or else another interrupt would occur immediately, causing the handler to be executed over and over again without ever returning to the main program. The handler clears the interrupt request immediately to give it time to take effect before leaving the handler.

How the address of the handler winds up in the vector table is not shown. The location of the vector table is held in the processor's VTOR register, whose contents may be accessed at address 0xE000ED08. If the table were located in read/write memory, then the initialization code of the main memory could modify the entry. However, the vector table is stored in non-volatile (read-only) memory so that once the program has been uploaded to the microcontroller, the table cannot be modified. However, it may be copied to read/write memory and the VTOR register updated accordingly.

```
#include <stdio.h>
#include <stdint.h>
#include "library.h"

#define TIM2_IRQ      28   // Timer 2 interrupt number
#define pTIM2_CR1     ((uint32_t *)  0x40000000)
#define pTIM2_DIER    ((uint32_t *)  0x4000000C)
#define pTIM2_SR      ((uint32_t *)  0x40000010)
#define pTIM2_CNT     ((uint32_t *)  0x40000024)
#define pTIM2_PSC     ((uint32_t *)  0x40000028)
#define pTIM2_ARR     ((uint32_t *)  0x4000002C)
#define pRCC_APB1ENR  ((uint32_t *)  0x40023840)
#define pNVIC_ISER0   ((uint32_t *)  0xE000E100)

volatile uint32_t tenths = 0 ;    // Counts tenths of a second
static   uint32_t previous = 0 ;  // Used to recognize a change

void TIM2_IRQHandler(void)  // Interrupt Handler
    {
    *pTIM2_SR &= ~1 ;       // Clear interrupt request
    tenths++ ;              // Increment tenths counter
    }

int main(void)
    {
    InitializeHardware(HEADER, PROJECT_NAME) ;

    *pRCC_APB1ENR |= 1 ;                    // Power up timer 2
    *pTIM2_PSC    = 18000 ;                 // Setup prescaler and reload
    *pTIM2_ARR    = 1000 - 1 ;              //  to interrupt 10 times/sec
    *pTIM2_DIER   = 1 ;                     // Enable timer to interrupt
    *pTIM2_CR1    = 1 ;                     // Enable timer to count
    *pNVIC_ISER0  = 1 << TIM2_IRQ ;         // Unmask timer interrupt
    asm ("cpsie i") ;                       // Enable interrupts

    while (1)
        {
        if (tenths == previous) continue ;
        printf("tenths = %u\n", (unsigned) tenths) ;
        previous = tenths ;
        }
    }
```

Listing 12-6 Program to demonstrate interrupts triggered by timer ticks.

A different approach was used to change the vector table entry for the program shown in Listing 12-6. The library source code includes "weak" definitions of default handlers. By writing your own function using the same function name, the weak handler is automatically replaced by your own when the executable image is built by the linker.

12.4 DIRECT-MEMORY ACCESS: MEMORY-TO-MEMORY TRANSFER

Direct memory access (DMA) uses a hardware controller that once configured through software, can transfer data independently of the processor and concurrent with its execution of instructions. DMA can transfer data from memory to a peripheral, from a peripheral to memory, or from one region of memory to another. Since no instructions are executed to transfer the data, the transfer rate is limited only by the speed of the memory and/or the peripheral and thus is the highest transfer rate that is possible.

To perform a transfer, the DMA controller must know the source, destination and number of items of data to transfer. When complete, it can alert the processor with an interrupt or the processor can use polling to wait until the number of items remaining to be transferred reaches zero. If the transfer is from memory to a peripheral, you would normally configure the controller to automatically increment the source address after each item is transferred. If the transfer is from a peripheral to memory, you would do the same for the destination address. And of course if the transfer is from one region of memory to another, then both the source and destination addresses should be incremented.

Listing 12-7 illustrates how to program the DMA controller to transfer a block of data from one region of memory to another. Transferring between memory and a peripheral is similar. There are two functions. An application program simply calls the first function to configure the controller and start the transfer. The application may then execute other code as desired, but should not use the data from the destination until calling the second function to confirm that no more items remain to be transferred.

```
#define pRCC_AHB1ENR    ((uint32_t *)           0x40023830)
#define pDMA_S0CR       ((uint32_t *)           0x40026410)
#define pDMA_S0NDTR     ((volatile uint32_t *)  0x40026414)
#define pDMA_S0PAR      ((void **)              0x40026418)
#define pDMA_S0M0AR     ((void **)              0x4002641C)

void DMASetUp(void *src, void *dst, uint16_t bytes)
    {
    *pRCC_AHB1ENR |= (1 << 22) ;         // Enable DMA Clock
    *pDMA_S0CR     = 0 ;                 // Disable DMA
    *pDMA_S0PAR    = src ;               // Setup source address
    *pDMA_S0M0AR   = dst ;               // Setup dest. address
    *pDMA_S0NDTR   = (uint32_t) bytes ;  // Setup byte count
    *pDMA_S0CR     = 0x681 ;             // Auto++, Mem-To-Mem, Go
    }

int DMABusy(void)
    {
    return *pDMA_S0NDTR != 0 ;           // remaining bytes?
    }
```

Listing 12-7 C functions for using the DMA to do a memory-to-memory transfer.

The initialization function begins by enabling the clock signal that drives the DMA controller, and then configures the operating parameters of the device. The operating parameters cannot be configured unless the controller is disabled. Once the parameters have been set, the DMA controller is enabled and the transfers begin. Note that enabling the controller to start the transfer can be done with the same line of code that sets other options in the DMA control register. Listing 12-8 is the same two functions, rewritten in assembly.

```
        .syntax        unified
        .cpu           cortex-m4
        .text
        .thumb_func
        .align         2

// void DMASetUp2(void *src, void *dst, uint16_t bytes)

        .global        DMASetUp2
DMASetUp2:
    PUSH  {R4}                    // Preserve R4

    LDR   R3,=0x40023800  // RCC_BASE
    LDR   R4,[R3,0x30]
    ORR   R4,R4,(1 << 22) // Enable DMA Clock
    STR   R4,[R3,0x30]

    LDR   R3,=0x40026400  // DMA2_BASE

    LDR   R4,=0          // Make sure DMA is disabled
    STR   R4,[R3,0x10]

    STR   R0,[R3,0x18]   // Setup src address
    STR   R1,[R3,0x1C]   // Setup dst address
    STR   R2,[R3,0x14]   // Setup byte count

    LDR   R0,=0x681      // Setup Autoincrement,
    STR   R0,[R3,0x10]   // Memory-To-Memory, Start

    POP   {R4}           // Restore R4
    BX    LR             // Return

// int DMABusy2(void)

        .global        DMABusy2
DMABusy2:
    LDR   R0,=0x40026400  // DMA2_BASE
    LDR   R0,[R0,0x14]    // Get remaining byte count
    BX    LR              // Return

    .end
```

Listing 12-8 Assembly functions for using the DMA to do a
memory-to-memory transfer.

12.5 THE CPU CLOCK CYCLE COUNTER

The following example is provided merely to show how one can measure the run time performance in CPU clock cycles and can be useful when trying to squeeze the last nanosecond of performance out of an assembly routine.

The STM32F429 processor has an internal clock cycle counter that is part of the "Data Watchpoint and Trace" (DWT) Unit. Once enabled, use the GetClockCycleCount function to read the number of elapsed clock cycles before and after executing your code. Their difference then provides the running time of the code. Note that the run-time library used in this text calls the StartClockCycleCounter function from inside the InitializeHardware function.

```
#define pDWT_CTRL    ((uint32_t *)  0xE0001000)
#define pDWT_CYCCNT  ((volatile uint32_t *)    0xE0001004)
#define pDEMCR       ((uint32_t *)  0xE000EDFC)

void StartClockCycleCounter(void)
    {
    *pDEMCR     |= (1 << 24) ; // Enable use of DWT regs (set bit 24)
    *pDWT_CTRL  |= (1 <<  0) ; // Enable the counter (set bit 0)
    }

uint32_t GetClockCycleCount(void)
    {
    return *pDWT_CYCCNT ;      // Read the counter
    }
```

Listing 12-9 C functions to control the CPU clock cycle counter.

CREATING AN EMBITZ PROJECT FROM SCRATCH

Like any IDE that supports several different target platforms, there are a lot of configuration options that have to be configured. The following steps are for those who want or need to create an application program from scratch for the STMicroelectronics 32F429I-DISCO Discovery kit. Though tedious, once done you can use **File > Save project as template…** to save the settings and reuse them to create a new project with the same settings much more easily using **File > New > From template …**

1. Open EmBitz and click **Create a new project** in the middle of the screen.

2. In the dialog box that opens, select the **STMicro-ARM** icon and click **Go**.

3. A "Welcome to the new STmicroelectronics …" dialog box labelled STmicro-ARM may open. To prevent it from opening again next time, click on the check box and then click **Next**.

4. Another dialog box labeled STMicro-ARM will open. Enter the name of your project in the **Project title** field. Enter the folder where you want to store your project in the field labeled **Folder to create project in**. The other two fields will complete automatically. If everything looks OK, click **Next**.

5. Another dialog box labeled STMicro-ARM will open. Accept the default settings, including the checked boxes to create of the Debug and Release configurations. Click on **Next.**

6. Another dialog box labeled STMicro-ARM will open. Select **Cortex-M4 (F3xx-F4xx)** and then click **Next.**

7. Another dialog box labeled STMicro-ARM will open. Select **STM32F4xx (Cortex M4 with FPU)** and then click **Next.**

8. Another dialog box labeled STMicro-ARM will open. Select **STM32F429ZI** from the pull-down list of processors. Change the **Stack size** to 0x0400 and the **Heap Size** to 0x0200 and then click **Finish.**

9. Two dialog boxes will appear, one on top (labeled ST-link | STMicroelectronics) of the other (labeled Debug interface options). Click **OK** on the top dialog box and again on the second dialog box.

10. In the **Management** pane of the main window, right click on the name of your project and select Remove files... A dialog box labeled Multiple Selection will open. Click **Select All** and then click **OK.** In the confirmation window that appears, click **Yes.**

11. In the main menu, click on **File** and then **New** and then **Empty file.**

12. A dialog box labeled Add file to project will open. Click **Yes.**

13. A dialog box labeled Save file will open. At the bottom of the box, select **All files (*.*)** in the pull-down list labeled Save as type. Use the mouse to select and then delete all files and folders shown **<u>except</u>** the file with the extension .ebp.

14. In the same dialog box, enter either a source code filename with an extension of .c (for a C file) or .s (for an assembly language file) and click **Save**. A small dialog box labeled Multiple selection will appear; click **OK**. A pane in the main window will appear, labeled with the filename you just entered. Type in the source code for that file.

15. Repeat steps 11-14 for each source code file that will be part of your project.

16. In the Management pane, right-click on the project name and select **Build Options...** from the drop-down list.

17. A dialog window named Project build options will open. There are several options to be configured in this window. Click on the project name in the upper left corner and then do the following:

18. Click on the **Compiler settings** tab.

    a. Click on the **C-Flags** tab. In the Others: pane, enter **–fno-strict-aliasing**.

    b. From the **Categories** pull-down list, select **Optimization**.

    c. Place a checkmark next to "**Optimization disabled [-O0]**"

    d. Scroll down to the last checkbox and place a checkmark next to "**Treat floating point constant as single precision constant (no double)**"

    e. Click on the **#defines** tab. Enter the following lines of text:

    ARM_MATH_CM4
    __FPU_USED
    STM32F429ZI
    STM32F4XX
    PROJECT_NAME=\"$(PROJECT_NAME)\"

19. Click on the **Linker settings** tab. Under the "**Linker flags**" sub-tab, click on the pull-down menu labelled "**Catego-ries**" and select "**Library selection**". Make sure that the boxes "Newlib Nano-branch" and "Use float printf with Nano-branch" are both checked.

20. Stay in **Linker settings** and click on the **Libraries** tab. Click on **Add**. In the Add library window that opens, click on the button labeled "**...**" and locate the file library.a, se-lect it and click **Open**. In the dialog box labeled Question that asks "Keep this as a relative path", click **Yes**. In the Add library window that opens, click **OK**.

21. Click on the **Search directories** tab. Click on the **Includes** tab, and then click **Add**. In the Add directory window that opens, click on the button labeled "**...**" and the locate the folder that contains the file library.h and click **OK**. In the dialog box labeled Question that asks "Keep this as a rela-tive path", click **Yes**. In the Add directory window that opens, click **OK**.

Note: The library archive file (library.a) was adapted from code developed and distributed by STMicroelectronics who requires that the following copyright notice be included in this distribution.

COPYRIGHT(c) 2015 STMicroelectronics
Redistribution and use in source and binary forms, with or without modification, are permitted provided that the following conditions are met:

1. Redistributions of source code must retain the above copyright notice, this list of conditions and the follow-ing disclaimer.

2. Redistributions in binary form must reproduce the above copyright notice, this list of conditions and the

following disclaimer in the documentation and/or other materials provided with the distribution.

3. Neither the name of STMicroelectronics nor the names of its contributors may be used to endorse or promote products derived from this software without specific prior written permission.

THIS SOFTWARE IS PROVIDED BY THE COPYRIGHT HOLDERS AND CONTRIBUTORS "AS IS" AND ANY EXPRESS OR IMPLIED WARRANTIES, INCLUDING, BUT NOT LIMITED TO, THE IMPLIED WARRANTIES OF MERCHANTABILITY AND FITNESS FOR A PARTICULAR PURPOSE ARE DISCLAIMED. IN NO EVENT SHALL THE COPYRIGHT HOLDER OR CONTRIBUTORS BE LIABLE FOR ANY DIRECT, INDIRECT, INCIDENTAL, SPECIAL, EXEMPLARY, OR CONSEQUENTIAL DAMAGES (INCLUDING, BUT NOT LIMITED TO, PROCUREMENT OF SUBSTITUTE GOODS OR SERVICES; LOSS OF USE, DATA, OR PROFITS; OR BUSINESS INTERRUPTION) HOWEVER CAUSED AND ON ANY THEORY OF LIABILITY, WHETHER IN CONTRACT, STRICT LIABILITY, OR TORT (INCLUDING NEGLIGENCE OR OTHERWISE) ARISING IN ANY WAY OUT OF THE USE OF THIS SOFTWARE, EVEN IF ADVISED OF THE POSSIBILITY OF SUCH DAMAGE.

APPENDIX B
GRAPHICS LIBRARY FUNCTIONS

The STMicroelectronics 32F429I-DISCO Discovery board features a full color graphics display. The library file (library.a) includes a number of graphics functions that are not declared in the corresponding include file (library.h). However, a second include file (graphics.h) is provided for those who may wish to develop graphics applications to run on the board.

The file graphics.h provides C function prototypes for the graphics library functions and a number of macro definitions to make using those functions a bit less tedious. To write a graphics program for the board, add the C preprocessor directive "#include "graphics.h" at the top of your C program and then access the graphics functions using the macro definitions listed below.

```
#define  XPIXELS  240      // left edge of screen is at x = 0
#define  YPIXELS  320      // top edge of screen is at y = 0

void SetColor(uint32_t Color)

uint32_t ReadPixel(uint16_t Xpos, uint16_t Ypos)

void DrawPixel(uint16_t Xpos, uint16_t Ypos, uint32_t pixel)

void ClearDisplay(uint32_t Color)

void ClearStringLine(uint32_t Line)

void DisplayStringAtLine(uint16_t Line, uint8_t *ptr)
```

void DisplayStringAt(uint16_t X, uint16_t Y, uint8_t *pText,
        int alignment)

void DisplayChar(uint16_t Xpos, uint16_t Ypos, uint8_t Ascii)

void DrawHLine(uint16_t Xpos, uint16_t Ypos,
        uint16_t Length)

void DrawVLine(uint16_t Xpos, uint16_t Ypos,
        uint16_t Length)

void DrawLine(uint16_t X1, uint16_t Y1, uint16_t X2,
        uint16_t Y2)

void DrawRect(uint16_t Xpos, uint16_t Ypos, uint16_t Width,
        uint16_t Height)

void DrawCircle(uint16_t Xpos, uint16_t Ypos,
        uint16_t Radius)

void DrawEllipse(int Xpos, int Ypos, int XRadius,
        int YRadius)

void DrawBitmap(uint32_t X, uint32_t Y, uint8_t *pBmp)

void FillRect(uint16_t Xpos, uint16_t Ypos, uint16_t Width,
        uint16_t Height)

void FillCircle(uint16_t Xpos, uint16_t Ypos, uint16_t Radius)

void FillTriangle(uint16_t X1, uint16_t X2, uint16_t X3,
        uint16_t Y1, uint16_t Y2, uint16_t Y3)

void FillEllipse(int Xpos, int Ypos, int XRadius, int YRadius)

APPENDIX C
TOUCH SCREEN LIBRARY FUNCTIONS

The STMicroelectronics 32F429I-DISCO Discovery board features a touch screen display. An include file (touch.h) is provided for those who may wish to develop graphics applications that use the touch screen. Follow the approach shown in Listing C-1.

```c
#include <stdio.h>
#include <stdlib.h>
#include "library.h"
#include "touch.h"

#define THRESHOLD   10

int main(void)
    {
    int oldX = 0, oldY = 0 ;

    InitializeHardware(HEADER, PROJECT_NAME) ;
    printf("Waiting for input...\n") ;
    while (1)
        {
        if (TS_Touched())
            {
            int x = TS_GetX() ;
            int y = TS_GetY() ;
            if (abs(x - oldX) > THRESHOLD || abs(y - oldY) > THRESHOLD)
                {
                printf("x,y=%d,%d\n", x, y) ;
                oldX = x ;
                oldY = y ;
                }
            }
        }
    }
```

Listing C-1 Example of how to use the touch screen library functions

INDEX